Song Over Silence

A STORY ABOUT FINDING MY VOICE WHILE HEALING CHILD INCEST ABUSE

A MEMOIR BY

JILL DYANN BITTLE

 FriesenPress

Suite 300 - 990 Fort St
Victoria, BC, V8V 3K2
Canada

www.friesenpress.com

Copyright © 2020 by Jill Dyann Bittle
First Edition — 2020

ISBN
978-1-5255-7041-4 (Hardcover)
978-1-5255-7042-1 (Paperback)
978-1-5255-7043-8 (eBook)

1. FAM001010 FAMILY & RELATIONSHIPS, ABUSE, CHILD ABUSE

Distributed to the trade by The Ingram Book Company

The soul has no secret that behavior does not reveal.

Lao Tzu

Song Over Silence is dedicated to all survivors of child incest or sexual abuse who have yet to find hope, healing, and happiness in their hearts. May you find your voice, reclaim your power with self-love, mend your story, and eventually craft a beautiful life. ❤

I am also dedicating this book to those living with any degree of autism, borderline personality disorder (BPD), complex post-traumatic stress disorder (CPTSD), anxiety, dissociative identity disorder, depression, and obsessive-compulsive disorder (OCD). You are warriors. ❤

FOREWORD

I felt compelled to write this book in the hopes young people and teens realize that speaking up should be their only choice if they are being preyed upon and to let them know they are worthy of love and protection. No child should ever have to endure a family predator forcing themselves on their precious body, especially in the name of love. As you can imagine, it damages a child's psyche and soul, and it is beyond painful in many ways: emotionally, mentally, physically, sexually, spiritually, psychologically, and psychosomatically.

Every minor has a legal right to shield themselves against this kind of trauma and should disclose the crimes to authorities. Telling can be hard if it is someone you love, but the family member is wrong to sexually abuse children, and they will keep hurting others if we do not stop them. Statistically, the average pedophile will abuse hundreds of times and never get caught, so you are likely not the only survivor. This is the most important message to any kids reading this book: if you, or anyone you know, is being secretly assaulted, tell a parent or someone you trust right away. The person hurting you is dangerous, and they need help, therapy, medication, or jail, depending on the crimes and circumstances.

Should you feel you might like to tell a doctor, school counselor, teacher, or principal, I also recommend doing this because they are trained professionals. Family members are not always best equipped to handle this sad truth, especially if it is a person they love. You must be brave, though, and do whatever it takes to escape the abuse before it destroys your happiness. Do not feel you have to keep the dirty secret in the name of family loyalties and pay the price with your sanity.

Furthermore, if you are an adult who has carried a shameful secret because of a family member's sexual abuse, I also encourage you to speak out and seek healing for the sacred wounds you carry. Your mental health likely depends on it. Please know you are worthy of love, supported here, and are not alone on your journey. ♥

CONTENTS

One

THE YOUNGER YEARS AND CHILDHOOD BLISS

My life began on Tuesday, April 17, 1973, after my mom's long and difficult delivery. I weighed in at seven pounds, nine ounces, and measured nineteen and a half inches long. My mom gifted me the names Jill, after a friend who sang in her teen choir, and Dyann. My sweet parents, BlueBell and Graham, filled with love, welcomed me into this crazy world and likely had big dreams to create a marriage and home life happier than the ones they had been raised in.

Mom's parents were religious, strict, decent, working-class people, but I am not sure they acknowledged my mom's extra-sensitive nature or had much time for her because of their careers. Dad's upbringing, however, was something else altogether. His home had been scary and chaotic because his dad was temperamental, hurtful, and often punishing in nature. Percy, the eccentric playboy patriarch, was also somewhat of a madman who demanded obedience and seemed to objectify the many beauties around him.

The family environment was hectic, and the stories were that the home had been overcrowded with seven unruly children who were impoverished growing up. They were so poor at times that all the kids got for Christmas one year was a pencil, and they went hungry a lot and often fought over food. My dad's father was a tyrant when he did not get his way but was also a glutton for good times, and he loved to fight for all the finest things in life. Grandpa had worked different jobs over the years, including military service in the Air Force during World War II, but he was not over-achieving otherwise until he stumbled into sales and started his own company in his forties.

Once my dad graduated high school he worked hard with his parents on their growing business, and they surprisingly amassed a strong, consistent fortune for the family. Naturally, the wealth created a ton of excitement at the time, but it also created a competitive environment of greed, jealousy, favoritism, shame, perversion, perfectionism, entitlement, and intimidating secrecy.

Most amazingly, despite all these hardships growing up, Graham and BlueBell had found a home in each other's hearts; they had me, and I had them, and that was the only thing that mattered to our newly formed family unit!

When I arrived into this world, my dad was twenty-one. He was the second-oldest child of his family, and he was funny, incredibly driven, romantic, openhearted, liberated, and a "dare the fates" kind of guy who considered himself lucky to have married his high school sweetheart. BlueBell had just turned twenty. She was sweet, rebellious, ideologically feminist, independent, musical, and had been divinely designated the most important role in my life: that of mother.

Of course, I have no recall for the first year of growing up, but eleven short months later my sister, Veronica, was born. I became the big sister, a title I hated, because I always was bigger in size. Mom called us her Irish twins because we were born less than twelve months apart, and our life was full. As our family needed more space with the new baby, my hippie-minded parents decided to move out of our apartment and into a small house in the country. It was here that they would spend the next six years raising us girls on a forty-acre homestead plot outside Winnipeg, Manitoba in Canada.

The farm they purchased was truly dreamy, and it had a charming white, two-story family home on a cement basement foundation. When you walked in the front door, you could step left to go down into the red, shag-carpeted basement, or up to the main level of the home. The decor was trendy, with 1970s palettes of burnt orange with gold and cream wallpaper. The kitchen had fancy built-in cupboards, an oblong table with matching chairs, and a black, rotary-dial phone mounted on the wall. The living room was cozy, and the south-facing picture windows were lovely. My parents' bedroom was across from the bathroom, and up two short, narrow flights of stairs were three small kids' rooms.

Outside there sat a summerhouse, a small barn for raising and slaughtering chickens, an iconic red horse barn with a hip-style roof, a garage, a couple sheds, a raised fuel-storage tank, and one massive weeping willow in the middle of the yard. There were mature trees surrounding the property, rows of planted evergreens, swing sets, and even some neighboring families with kids. During this period, my mom's parents also moved into the nearby town, and I liked having them live close to us. They were super loving and caring grandparents and a hard-working couple who had raised three beautiful girls together.

My Grandma Lydia was exceptionally bright and had even challenged herself to go back to university in her forties to gain a master's degree in education, something that was highly unusual for the time, but that the women in our family were always so proud of. Her husband, William, adored her, and he would do anything to please her. As a couple, they were passionate about gardening, making homemade bread, soups, or baking desserts, and hanging out together. Time with these two was special, and we adored them. Grandpa Bill was sweet, and we loved going to Sunday school with him or eating sweet treats together. He spoke exceptionally soft, was trustworthy and playful, and truly represented everything a good grandpa should be.

During the next few years, while my dad built his family's growing empire, my mom spent her time nurturing and playing with us girls and making sure our many needs were met. We mostly had fun together, but I struggled with temper tantrums, and this was tough for my mom because my sister never behaved that poorly. In fact, my mom often laughed at my dramatic nature because of the ridiculousness of my extreme displays of over-emotionality. Even from a young age this would enrage me, and I would stomp away in a fury. Honestly, I never liked cooperating with authority, being told what to do, tight or scratchy clothes, and the numerous daily demands to behave. Even at the tender age of three, I found this to be exhausting, and at times of impulsivity, impossible. Moreover, I felt scolded all the time for not listening, but the truth was, I just couldn't.

I remember being a messy and hyperactive child who seemed to have a serious side and a silly side, with little room for the range of feelings in between opposite ends of that spectrum. Often Mom would spend the days trying to control my wild spirit with her endless rules, but when Dad came home, he allowed me to be more of my wild self. I appreciated this accepting part of him that tolerated and loved me unconditionally the way only he did. My dad was a man who gladly took me under his wing anytime he saw I needed support or teaching, and I loved that. Dad also made everything fun, and he had an impressive imagination for adventure, magic, and storytelling.

He was mostly sweet and loved nursery rhymes and singing us children's songs: "Humpty Dumpty," "On Top of Spaghetti," "Farmer in the Dell," and "Kookaburra Sits in the Old Gum Tree" were a few of his favorites to sing and recite around the farm. As a dad, he would do anything to keep Veronica and me happy and loved to have fun with us. He was also a soft soul who would forever try to keep the peace in our house at any cost. He treasured the little family he created and tried hard not to carry forward the mistakes of his horrible father. Growing up around a storm of abuse impacted my dad though, and on temperamental occasions he lashed out to hurt me when pushed past his usual reasonable limits.

I can still vividly recall when I was horsing around one night, at about age four, and pushing my dad so hard that he broke through some drywall. Then, as if this were not enough,

I accidentally slammed Veronica's tiny fingers in the bathroom door a short time later and made them bleed. Well, my dad was livid, and he started screaming irately in my face and grabbing at me as I ran up the stairs to avoid his punishment. These interactions were upsetting to both of us, of course, but we never seemed to stay mad, and the rest of the time we got along fabulously. Forgive and forget, you know? He was my favorite person growing up, and I always knew I could count on him to help navigate the riffs between me and Veronica or my mom. He understood me and would reason with me instead of fighting with me, and this was a quality I truly adored.

Additionally, as a young girl I was a loud, bossy tomboy who loved playing outside, climbing trees and riding on any kind of equipment with my dad. I had a great affection for animals and have been obsessed with music, dancing, reading, and delicious food my whole life. Reading was definitely my favorite activity, because I enjoyed the imaginary world of the pages that I could visually fall into so easily. Mom has said I taught myself to read at a noticeably young age and went through every book I could get my little hands on. I was also a sweet, funny girl who delighted in playing in my tree house, humming, running around on my tiptoes, and splashing in the ditches to catch frogs or tadpoles. I felt filled with love, song, and laughter. I was free and happy, even if I could not always make sense of the spinning world around me. I managed because I had loving parents, but life often seemed like a blur of irritating noises, bright lights, and things and people I either liked, or likely ignored.

During these younger years, my dad worked exhaustively during the week, while us girls followed our daily routine around the house, which included mealtimes, bath times, and bedtimes. Veronica and I would play as mom did the chores, and in her spare time, Mom liked to talk on the telephone, listen to records, and sit at the kitchen table with a friend or sister, smoking cigarettes, chatting, laughing, and drinking coffee. Sometimes, my mom would invite relatives or neighbors over, so we had other children to play with. This was usually fun, unless kids teased me or upset me, and then I would be left in tears. People often called me a poor sport because of this, but really, I was just beyond hypersensitive.

Mom always made sure we participated in all the holiday traditions throughout the year, and she would make fun plans to celebrate with family or friends. One of my favorite young childhood memories was the Halloween my mom dressed me as Raggedy Ann. Also, our birthdays were extra special occasions, and we celebrated with only the newest decoration ideas of the time. Mom would go full out and shower Veronica, myself, or our dad with a day of love, a party, a fancy cake, and thoughtful presents. I felt like we were lucky to have her kindness and that she cared for us as much as she did.

By the age of five, society dictated that I was ready to leave the protection of the nest and branch out into the real world. In September 1978, my mom dressed me in my best red dress, a pair of black-and-white patent-leather shoes, and a button-down white cardigan, readying me for class. Armed with a lunch box and a backpack full of new school supplies on my shoulders, I happily skipped down our long driveway with Mom and Veronica. There, parked at the end, was a big yellow school bus, and I posed for first-day-of-kindergarten photos and went bravely to face a bunch of kids and a teacher I had never met. Ms. M proved to be kind, and the kids seemed okay, I guessed.

Except I did not like the one boy named Darcy who kissed my cheek behind the art easel. I thought it was inappropriate, and I certainly did not want to be his girlfriend.

Grade 1 proved harder, because the teacher was mean and scolded me constantly. One noon hour a pop had blown up in my lunch bag and ruined everything. She was angry for the mess, quickly threw out the wet food, and told me to get outside for lunch hour. I was horrified and starving, but I will tell you, this woman had zero patience for teaching and was regularly rude. Thankfully for me, this was the last year at the elementary school before we packed up our belongings and our white pet rat named Bigalo and moved into a mobile home on my dad's brand-new farm. He was proudly branching out on his own with a few large barns and a feed mill, leaving the family business behind.

Two

A NEW FARM, THE TRIP, AND FEAR

The acreage acquired had a small swimming hole, which we loved, and my dad wanted everything there to be perfect. He bought us a little three-wheeler to rip around on, matching princess bedroom furniture for both girls, a dog, and even a couple of Shetland ponies. A red mare named Flicka was mine, and a black female named Black Beauty belonged to Veronica. As for extra activities, my dad liked to camp outside in a tent with us, skate on the pond, scuba dive, and shoot guns, and he would often teach us how to be rough and tough like boys. Dad would say to Veronica and me, "Anything boys can do, girls can do better," and I believed this to be a pretty great motto for the time. You see, my dad was a feminist, and he wanted us to be independent and absolutely equal to, or better than, any man.

Grade 2 at my new school was fine, and the teacher found me responsible enough that I was granted the task of helping a teenage boy who suffered from epilepsy put on his helmet every morning. One day, however, as I went to do up his chin strap, he had a seizure, fell over, and sliced his head on the corner of a metal filing cabinet. In horror, I ran to the office with all my might, and medical help was called. I think other arrangements were made for his safety after that morning, but in hindsight, I am not sure a seven-year-old was mature enough to handle this very adult situation.

This was also the school year, during spring break of 1981, my parents decided that after ten years of marriage, they needed a holiday; maybe a second honeymoon. They were thrilled with the travel plans, but I was nervous, as I was not used to being away from them for any extended period of time. Arrangements had already been finalized with my paternal grandparents to care for me and Veronica at their home while our parents vacationed, and they were excited! As we prepped for the trip, our parents packed their suitcases alongside ours, and at the start of the holidays we made the twenty-five-minute drive to my dad's parents.

I absolutely adored my loving Grandma Sophia, but Percy, my Jekyll-and-Hyde grandfather would at times lash out at her in fits of maniacal rage, and I hated being around his abuse. It was loud and scary, and you just never knew what might happen, especially if he had been drinking. I witnessed a lot of it growing up, and I felt sorry for my grandma. When he was not acting out, grandpa pretended to be a "good guy," so he was definitely odd.

As my parents dropped me and Veronica off, kissed us goodbye, and wished us a fun week, my tiny heart filled with dread. This was going to be seven unbearably long days without them; a week that would permanently change my life…

I consciously remembered little things like trying to avoid my grandpa's wet kisses or his groping hands, dodging him during bathroom breaks, hiding before bedtime bible stories, car rides with grandpa, and the fear that would wash over me when darkness fell. I tried to wake my grandma one night, but the sleeping pills next to the bed may have rendered her unresponsive. During the week I would wake up dazed, confused, anxious, and angry, but had no idea why. I was beyond upset with worry the entire time, and I wished my parents were home. I wanted to tell my mom Grandpa was bad or write her a letter. My body felt like it was on fire, my brain felt endangered, and I was desperate to escape these panicky, painful feelings.

The evening our parents returned to pick us girls up, I desperately ran down the blue-carpeted stairs and threw my arms around my mom's right leg the second she walked through the front door. Smalltalk was made as we grabbed our bags, hurriedly jumped in the car, and headed back to the safety of our life that home had always provided. My parents were happy for the break, but my behavior would continue to spiral down for many years to follow, and for no apparent reason. My family and I did not have a clue how to control my constant miserable moods, and nobody ever knew what was wrong with me. I did not know what was wrong with me.

Coincidentally, I fell really sick after the homecoming, and Mom took me to our pediatrician, Dr. Armstrong. He had me tested and confirmed that I had mononucleosis, famously known as the "kissing disease." The doctor jokingly asked who I had been kissing. I hung my head in embarrassment and was dead silent. The adults laughed the joke off, but because my spleen was enlarged and I was alarmingly ill, Mom promised to keep me from school as long as it took to heal. With that, we went home, and after a few weeks of lying on the couch and avoiding what surely felt like death, I was back to my usual, full-spirited self, but with a trailblazing fire raging from within.

One evening, a short time after my recovery, Veronica and I started viciously scrapping in the hall as our parents were "stealing kisses" in their locked bedroom. They told us to go away but we were unable to listen because tempers were flaring. Frustratingly, in a fit, my dad flung open the door, grabbed each of us girls by one arm, and shoved us out on the front steps in our nighties and locked it behind him. We screamed and Mom immediately let us in, but I hated it when he got that angry. This punishing behavior would often escalate when traveling in the car because Veronica and I would fight relentlessly. When we did not stop, Dad would yank on my ponytail, pinch my knee or arm to get me to listen, or threaten to leave us on the side of the road. I never liked the hurt or the hard feelings these interactions caused, but they did not happen that often, so they were forgivable.

That year was extra hard for me. I was becoming increasingly fearful of the dark, defiant towards my family, and started having reoccurring nightmares about a purple monster lifting the roof off my house, or being caught or tortured and killed, and I developed a weird phobia of mice. I felt like a little grownup in a kid's world and did not know why. I was deeply lonely, sad, and painfully uncomfortable—a crawling-out-of-my-skin kind of discomfort. I wanted to be loved, but I did not like being too close to anyone, so it was a tough balance. I struggled to connect to other children, and even though I made friends, I continued to relate to adults better. It seemed at the time that I behaved well at school for my teachers but would then get increasingly self-isolating and grumpy towards Veronica and Mom in the evenings.

This pattern was getting extremely tiring, and finally, after spending a couple long years in the mobile, we again packed up our personal belongings. We moved into an architectural dream home overlooking a man-made lake and I was in heaven. I figured maybe this could be it—my fresh start, and a hope to leave behind everything that had ever hurt me.

Three

MY FRESH START AND DELIGHTFUL MEMORIES

The new home was amazing, and I loved it. When you first stepped into the lake house, all you could see were full-sized, wood-framed windows and patio doors that led out to a deck overlooking a beautiful lake. The front entrance, the walls of the formal dining room, and a mirrored telephone booth were spray-foamed to look like the interior of a white cave, which was cool. There was a spiral staircase with black chains as spindles and a "bridge" that wiggled as we ran across to the upstairs. My parents' room faced west and had twenty-four-foot-tall windows and curtains to match, with a view of the forest. Their room also had a built-in, king-sized waterbed, fancy his-and-hers dressing rooms with a shower in between, and windows that faced the often-sparkly lake to the south.

The main bathroom was lined with black-and-white wallpaper, which had bizarre pictures of half-naked cherubs. Off the dining area was a large, peaked living room that had rough lumbered walls halfway up and dark-brown cork to the top where the three skylights were. There were a few extra-large cants across the ceiling, and the focal point of the room was a massive brick fireplace on the east wall. The history was that the bricks had been reclaimed from our old provincial parliament building, but nonetheless, they had likely been chosen for their stunning beauty. The south wall had large picture windows and short, built-in bookcases, also made of the rough lumber. The attached kitchen was U-shaped and had orangey-red wallpaper with floating women and knights on horses. Also connected to the kitchen were a boot room and a large triple-car garage, which completed the main level. Dad had an Olympic-sized pool table in there that we played, and the space sometimes doubled as a party shack when he had staff parties or company.

The second level of the home was my favorite. Passed the bridged staircase was a small living room with a tall, custom bookshelf made from unfinished wood. Plus, there was a solarium facing south, with a walkout balcony. This was the best view in the house. To the right of these rooms were a bathroom and a kids peaked-roof bedroom that had a metal ladder up to a dream play loft to fill with toys. There were odd-shaped walk-in closets on each side of the room and a pedestal sink near the window. Perhaps the feature I loved the most was the large vines and big pink flower painted up the tall, slanted wall where my bed would find its final resting place. The last room on the second floor was the one with the secret door. One wall had all vertically installed wood planks, and if you pushed on the right board, this big door would open up to a small bedroom that had a railing to look over into the master living room.

Our family moved our furniture in, and my mom decorated this place to perfection. She appreciated a clean, calm, and quiet house and worked hard to keep things in order. My mom was a great cook, a supportive wife, and a seemingly natural mother. She managed everything related to the home and exhausted hours cleaning, laundering, shopping, and running us girls into the city for appointments and lessons. She spent most of her days alone while Dad was building his empire and funding his house full of girls. Mom loved homemaking and being in charge of her own family. She also adored motherhood and being Graham's wife. Together, they modeled a caring marriage, and it appeared they were especially important to each other. Their life was nice, and I even imagined I wanted that kind of loving marriage when I grew up.

My mom was not afraid to do yard work or the tougher jobs around the house because we lived in the country and my dad was away working a lot. She was strong-willed, independent, and always on the go with new projects. Mom was a woman who knew what she wanted and worked tirelessly to achieve her goals. I am certain she did not have an easy time with these many responsibilities, but she did them like a boss and was consistently very well composed and polite. Her parents had raised a good girl, and it always showed.

We spent the next few years enjoying the lake life, going to school, swimming, and attending summer bible camps with our friends. The big holidays were always happily spent with my dad's wildly fun side of the family, hanging out and making gourmet holiday meals for dozens of relatives. I loved our extended family of aunts and uncles, and the abundance of cousins and special times they brought into my life. We also did lots of traveling with my parents and often went to fancy work conventions throughout Canada with our paternal grandparents for entertainment.

During the summer, of course, we loved spending time at my Grandma Sophia's backyard pool with a bunch of kids, teasing, playing, and challenging each other in any way possible. This was fun, plus it was common for my grandma to invite half the neighborhood to swim, and those hot, summer days were a blast! Veronica and I participated in Pioneer Girls Club, and I loved acting in Christmas concerts and singing in school plays. I enjoyed doing any winter activities and endlessly reading for hours and playing in my room alone. The other cabins surrounding our house were mainly seasonal campers, so there would be a handful of families to play with during school breaks, but for most of the year the area was without children. My mom was great about letting us have friends come over for sleepovers on weekends during the school year, but it involved lots of driving people around, and it was not always practical.

Veronica and I spent much of our time together growing up, and at times it was fun, but we had a strained relationship and tended to argue or fight. Of course, there were no cell phones or computers with internet to entertain us, so we were hard to be around. We had three TV channels when we lived in the country, and that was it. If any of us wanted to telephone a friend, we would have to wait for the party line that was shared with a handful of neighbors to be free or listen in mischievously till it was. Luckily for my mom, our dad was good about taking us out skiing or going on adventures, building science-fair projects, or playing board games with us on the weekends and evenings to keep us entertained. He was a great dad and would help Mom wear us out whenever he was home.

Grade 4 proved a fun year for me because my friend Laura and I had built a big volcano project that won us a red ribbon and our picture in the local newspaper. It was a first real "win" in my history, and I reveled in childhood pride. Some of the only unfavorable memories for the year were having to get glasses and wearing a retainer to start correcting my underbite, which I did not like. In Grade 5, my dad helped me and another friend, Sadie, with our science-fair project about a farming topic, and to our surprise we won again. Except this time, we managed to go all the way to the Provincial Exhibition, where the project was a hit, and I won my first ever gold metal. Winning felt good, and we went on to repeat that same success the following years.

I loved competing, because my dad instilled that in me, and when it came to the chocolate bar sales for fundraising, no one could top us. I remember a year when we had sold enough bars to win one of the first ever Sony Walkmans. It was exciting technology back then, and I was in musical heaven. During class, I would sometimes excuse myself just to head to the bathroom and rock out to a quick blast of Pat Benatar, or Joan Jett on cassette, as it seemed far more fun than listening to the school curriculum.

In the seventh grade, my mom's parents moved close to us again because my sister Lily would be born, and my Grandma Lydia was going to retire to help mom with our new baby. This was a fun time for the family, and we all adored Lily. I was hopeful one day we could be friends. The kind of closeness that Veronica and Mom shared, maybe? They seemed to get along naturally, and I felt like the odd man out because I did not "get" them. I had always envied their connection, and I wanted a close friendship like that with somebody one day. So, I hoped I could get the sister thing right this time, as I had rarely been a particularly good one to Veronica.

Four

ENTER HORMONES AND BULLYING

1985 was the year I had just turned thirteen, and for hormonal reasons I started to take a huge interest in boys. Some liked me back, of course, but then I would change my mind and pick another boy to like. I had a few good friends, and I was giggly and hyper, but probably far too dramatic for my conservative homeroom teacher. He was considered a "perv" by a group of the older girls I knew and was one of those gym teachers that was way too friendly. Mr. G presented a lesson to our home-room one day and got our group started on math worksheets. Then, halfway through the class, he announced that he needed to speak with me. *What could he possibly want?* I thought.

He walked me down to a storage room that was staged like an interrogation chamber and closed the door. There was a chair, and the only light was from an overhead projector in front of me. He told me to sit down, then stood over me, breathing heavily, and started to ask me questions about why I was acting so "sexually seductive" at school. I had no clue what he was even talking about or why he was so serious about this topic. He released me after maybe ten minutes, but I found the encounter extremely creepy. I later mentioned this scenario to an older friend, Brigette, and she said he had done the same thing to her.

Grade 8 started fine, as I enjoyed fundraising, going for lunch with friends, and working in the school canteen, but then a series of negative events transpired throughout the year that would change my thirteen-year-old life. Sex and sexuality were not openly talked about in our small Christian community, and the only thing I ever heard was that any deviation from "straight" was sinful. Of course, in those days, everything was a sin. It is how the religious community attempted to control their "bad" children, or so it seemed to me, anyway. As we entered our first year of high school, it appeared that mostly the naughty teens were having sex, and only the boys were willing to talk about it. I thought more like the boys, plus I had also been secretly attracted to girls since I was young, and my curiosities were stirring.

However, only a boyfriend was socially acceptable at the time, so my flirtations were being thrown in that direction. I liked the boys' attention, even though I had little clue what to do with it once I got it. Of course, I knew about sex because I had skimmed through hidden pornography collections when I was younger, listened in on some 1-900 calls, and had read about the wild sex lives of the saucy characters in a naughty book. Mostly people called sex love or fun, but was it? Apparently, I was not ready for any kind of sex or closeness with boys yet, but

I was learning about the dance from a distance. I liked the idea of being sexy and felt mostly confident trying to be a young adult, even though I was still in the hugely late bloomer stage. I wanted to grow up already and smoke cigarettes, swear, be a rebel, party, and have a boyfriend to love me. I even went as far as having pretend cocaine in my purse that Halloween to appear "cool," but my friends probably thought it was devilish.

Just for shits and giggles, my one-year-older girl friend and I made out on a couple occasions. We were playful and considered it practice for when we got a boyfriend. It seemed fun and was fine, but I considered it a huge secret at the time. I will never know for sure, but I suspect Sadie naively mentioned it to another girl in our group, and shortly after, I was exiled for what the good girls likely viewed as "heathen" behavior. They wrote me a nasty letter detailing my spoiled and wicked ways, all signed it, and had my friend Kenneth deliver it right before "Oh Canada" one morning. I read it and instantly wanted to die of embarrassment or melt into the floor, and I was devastated. This is a moment that is seared into my memory bank, and one that would change everything about me.

As if getting dumped by the girls was not enough, Roxy, Demi, Jenna, and Sadie started bullying me and turning people in the high school against me for most of the year. Seriously, it was a true teenage nightmare, and I chose to turn the pain inward and became increasingly sad and self-loathing. I hated myself, and I would cry to my mom about the bullying, but I forbade her from speaking to anyone else about it. Not the teachers, not the principal, not the parents of the bullies. No one. It was my secret, and not hers to share. At the time, I never had any access to a counselor or spoke with a doctor regarding my struggles, and I continued to suffer in silence.

In May of 1987, I started the baseball season as usual, but a few games in, my right leg was accidentally twisted and broken in four places. I was rushed into emergency surgery to straighten and cast the injury and spent the next month lying in the hospital bed, plus three more months in a cast from toe to hip. I hated every minute of it. Mom gave birth to my baby sister Rosie during my hospital stay, and even with the excruciating pain I was in, I desperately looked forward to going home to my parents and sisters. I was extra lonely for my mom and found it hard to be in the hospital without her support.

When I went back to finish Grade 8, my four old friends decided to be friendly towards me again because of breaking my leg, which was a huge relief. I guess it was a decent way to end the year in this small town, but my new school was already selected, and I had been accepted to a prominent co-ed boarding school, for the fall. I was excited about moving to Winnipeg, because I seriously thought I might die spending any more time in a town that I considered so restrictive.

My summer had been good enough, but before it ended, Jenna and I played a dumb prank of putting hot peppers on an ice cream, which hurt two-year-old Lily. Well, my dad completely lost it; he dragged me out of the restaurant, threw me up against the car, and with his knees and arms flailing, he screamed, "I will f**cking kill you if you ever do that again!" Of course, he did not mean it, but what is said in anger cannot be undone, and I was triggered; horrified and the event sadly caused me hurt feelings against my dad for the next seven years. I knew he had been treated like that as a child, but it was scary, and I felt deeply ashamed to be so publicly humiliated. Honestly, I felt more betrayed by his words than his actions, and simply decided I was better off on my own. I figured if I were not close to anyone, no one could hurt me. This may seem drastic, but my thinking has always been this black and white.

Five

FREEDOM, HIGHER EDUCATION, AND EMOTIONAL CHAOS

In September 1987, me and a roommate were assigned to a small room in an old mansion, at the boarding school on the river and settled in. The city move seemed thrilling and was hopefully the fresh start I desperately needed. Perhaps I could find happiness, close friendships, and even love. My roommate, Macey, was friendly, and the other girls on the third floor seemed nice too. With a fresh perm, pink glasses, and a slight limp from the leg cast being removed, I was there and grateful for the experience of being in a place where education was a priority and girls were valued. My mom and dad had raised a strong-minded daughter, and this school provided an exceptional environment for my higher learning. I found it challenging, though, because I was not a natural student and had to work extra hard at the university-preparatory school.

The teachers there were compassionate and well educated, and they really took the extra time to explain and generously help me catch up on lessons I had previously been lacking. The class sizes at the time were sixteen to twenty pupils, with a 1:4 ratio of girls to boys, and everyone appeared incredibly social, knowledgeable, funny, intelligent, and interactive. Needless to say, I was beyond excited to be living with other boarding students, teachers, and housemasters, and enjoyed the other city kids that attended the school as well. It was a wonderful opportunity to step away from the bubbled world I had grown up in and a chance to better my poor-quality social skills.

The year consisted of regimented meals, classes, studying, exercise, weekends, and breaks. I thrived on the basic routines, and by the end of the year, I had made lots of new friends. I felt good, and that summer, at fifteen, I was finally beginning to look more like a woman than a girl. Of course, I loved my new curves, but it was also hard, because boys and men of all ages began to take a huge sexual interest in me. I didn't mind the attention from the boys I liked but hated the old and married men who would flirt, hit on, grope, assault, and make suggestive comments. So many of them were willing to have an affair with a fifteen-year-old girl, but this was remarkably prevalent at the time. I quickly became hyper-vigilant about steering clear of predatory men, but I was more naive with the boys and certainly experienced quite an abundance of sexual harassment.

In the summer of 1988, my paternal grandparents were heading west to visit my aunt, and they had invited me and a younger relative Larry, to spend a couple weeks on holiday.

It sounded fun, so we packed up our gear, made the twelve-hour drive to Edmonton with Grandpa Percy at the wheel, and enjoyed the vacation working in my aunt's cafe. The trip went by fast, and soon it was over. Somewhere on the long ride home, Larry and I were acting way too silly and singing and joking around in the back seat of the car. While this sounds harmless, the problem was we were driving Grandpa mad, and when Larry would not stop to Grandpa's liking, he erupted. In typical fashion, he started driving faster and erratically, then quickly pulled into the first motel he could find. He marched straight into the front desk and rented two rooms, side by side. One for the girls and a suite for the boys. My stomach sank because I knew exactly what kind of trouble Larry was in, but who could I tell, and what would I even say? Plus, I had no access to a phone. Well, my grandfather raged like a lunatic for the next hour, and we could hear yelling and things being scuffled around. It was disturbing to listen to, but eventually it stopped, and the night fell completely silent.

We loaded up the car the next morning and acted like the night had not happened, but this was absolutely typical. (Ignoring this abuse from our paternal grandfather and sanitizing its severity was lifelong, and nobody ever dared speak against the disgusting toxicity of his madness. If you did, you were in danger of punishment, or of being on the wrong end of one of his explosive verbal outbursts.)

As I started Grade 10, I managed to talk my mom into getting me contacts, grew out my hair longer, and I felt more social. I was also gaining self-esteem and popularity, which I so desperately wanted. I got my driver's license, which was pure heaven, and I worked a couple of jobs for extra money. High school was entertaining, and I delighted in going to parties, theatre performances, ballets, concerts, and hanging out with boy crushes or other friends. There was much to do in the city, and I appreciated that. In fact, I rarely went home to my family because I would make other plans for myself. The sad truth was I felt disconnected from them, and I stubbornly kept everybody pushed away because it seemed easier than trying to get along. Plus, I was still mad at my dad, Veronica seemed like she was always trying to control me, and my mom was drowning in babies. Needless to say, home felt chaotic at the time, and I avoided it as much as I could.

In Grade 11, my mom and younger sisters moved a couple hours away to be with my dad at his new 3200-acre farm, and they left our lake home to sit empty for the next few years. It was a good move for mom and the girls, but they now appeared even more out of reach to me because I did not like to drive that far. However, I still went back to our lake home on many weekends just to have the quiet place to myself. It was lonely without them, but it was a comfortable space, and I loved the safety it had always provided.

Many of the girls that attended the prestigious private school were well controlled, "proper," and incredibly smart, but for whatever reason I viewed a lot of them as competition. I tried to act and look like them, but I never believed I was as "perfect" as the popular girls, and I was obsessively hard on myself for this. Mostly I found hanging out with groups of boys easier, because they were more accepting of my rowdiness and sometimes social or sexual inappropriateness. I also found it tough to date any boy long term because I had, as one quoted, "commitment issues." I did not even understand what that meant at seventeen, but it sounded about right. As soon as a guy I liked would try to get too close to me, I would flee like the whole place was on fire. It was a pattern I could not get a handle on, and it caused me a lot of distress. I was bouncing around with many different friends and groups and trying to figure out who I needed to be to be liked; looking to belong, but never really feeling like I fit in. Everyone else mingled comfortably and effortlessly. I, however, hid my anxiousness and was hypercritical of myself when I would endure what I regarded as mistakes or personal and relationship failures.

I also struggled with poor decision-making, impulsivity, hypersexuality, undiagnosed depression, social anxiety, and OCD. I secretly battled my thoughts on a daily basis but never spoke of it to anyone. Grades, weight, looks, and boy, family or friend troubles, or any slight comment, could all send me into a tailspin on most days, and I felt out of control. I was stressed and eating to cope or dieting to shed the pounds, which then created some very disordered eating rules or restrictions, as well as body dysmorphia. The charts at the time said that at 5'6" I should be 120 pounds, and my natural weight liked sitting at 160 pounds. So, any smaller size was impossible to maintain. I carried a lot of shame about these feelings but did my best to keep them buried. I was, after all, a perfectionist in training, and taking the job quite seriously.

I became obsessed with trying to look good, and if I did anything wrong, I would punish myself with the wickedest self-talk. Or I would act out in other ways, such as scratching my skin, dying or chopping off my hair, overhauling my appearance, getting a new tattoo, engaging in self-piercing, or making regretful, impulsive choices, and would then self-chastise for being such an idiot. It seemed like a cycle, and one I was trying to get a handle on. I struggled because I could not consistently act like a loyal partner, sister, or girlfriend, or figure out how to maintain long-term relationships without getting too close and then ultimately feeling suffocated. I craved intimacy, but only on my terms. I was like a social butterfly, never wanting to be caught, and so I was forever on the move. I dated one boy for the eleventh school year but dumped him in the end because I found the relationship demands tedious and boring. Especially his need for constant eye contact, which he told me I was not very good at.

It was our graduation year in the fall of 1990, and as seniors, we were exhilarated to move back into the newly renovated second floor of the manor. The Grade 12 suite had a large main room with three beds, a side room with two bunks, and a fantastic sunroom facing west with a couple more beds. I quickly tossed my belongings onto the sunniest one. I was looking forward to having my newly acquired prefect privileges, and to meet the newest boarding students. In the side quarters was my dear friend, Annie, and a new, bubbly international student named Holly, who was a year older than us. She was brilliant, beautiful, and it appeared she had set her sights on me from day one, and for the rest of the year we were perfectly inseparable.

We shopped, went for drives, partied, played pranks, ate, smoked, and giggled the nights away talking about wankers, shagging, snogging, and handsome blokes. We had no filters together, and we loved being loud, making sex jokes, being obnoxious, and laughing at everything we could. Holly had the wickedest sense of humor, and she was famous for writing me the wildest pretend love letters from Great Britain on the school breaks. By the end of the year we were the best and closest of friends, and when it came time to say goodbye, it was heart-breaking for me, because I felt like I would never see the dearest friend I had ever had again. This was a hard loss, but grow up, right? Time to get on with adult life.

Six

UNIVERSITY BOUND
AND UNPLANNED PREGNANCY

I spent that summer living at the lake house and working at the local beach canteen, and in the fall of 1991, I started university. When I got there, I had been assigned to a top-floor room in the very southern corner of the eight-story cement building. Of course, I did not know anyone, so I was both nervous and excited about assimilating into a campus setting. In my room there was a tiny window, basic desk, and single bed. It looked ridiculously depressing but so be it. I had not had a space to myself since I was eight, and to be honest, I was not sure I even liked the idea. The only plus here was that as part of my boarding package, I was given a meal card that allowed for three choices a day from the cafeteria, and it was nice to not have to worry about preparing meals as a student.

I loved the courses I chose, and even had some guys I graduated with in a few of my classes, so I was glad for that. It looked like all the girls in my grad class had headed off to distant universities, so I knew very few people at the school. Psychology, political science, English, anthropology, and sociology were on my first-year agenda, and I wanted to learn as much about people as I could. I thought maybe it could help me. University of Manitoba was a large campus, and if I were to survive, I would surely have to make the most of blending in with this new crowd of students. I guess I did mostly fine there and managed to make a few friends in my residence to party with, but we were not what I would call close, and it left me feeling unsettled.

As the first semester ended, I was socially exhausted, super stressed, increasingly depressed, and was making extremely poor decisions. It was a lonely few months of trying to feel connected to anyone when I realized this dorm life was not going to work for me. I was in sensory overload, and I was irritable. It was too loud, unpredictable, not at all private, and it seemed nearly impossible to get a good night's sleep there. The partying was a real headache for my social anxiety, and as I hated drinking, I often felt out of place, tired, or uncomfortable.

It happened my mom mentioned this to my aunt, and she generously offered me a room in her basement. I immediately jumped at the opportunity, because I had always adored her. My mom's sister was a wise woman and had been really kind to me growing up. She was supportive, relaxed, unconventional, affectionate, and was a successful realtor who had two cats and was living with a much-younger man at the time. Her home was small, but it was happy and comfortable, and the older cat,

Phoenix, took to sleeping with me, which helped a little with the ferocious loneliness I was experiencing.

I managed to finish the last semester but ended up falling just below the 60% required to further advance in my desired field of psychology. I was ashamed of this failure but quickly registered to major in political science, and minor in English, plus a few classes in chemistry, philosophy, and world religions for the following year. I was off for the summer anyway. I spent it working at a pizza restaurant and lounge in a small town and enjoyed living in the lake house. I had a fun red sports car that my grandpa Percy had bought for me, and I loved the freedom to be able to drive anywhere I wanted. (As the oldest grandchild, he had always spoiled me with close affections and special gifts.)

Sometimes I would go to socials or parties for fun, but mostly I spent time alone at the house or in the company of a current boy crush or girlfriend. It was a great, stress-free summer and a much-needed two-month break from university. I felt refreshed at the end of the season and was praying for better luck socially, mentally, and academically for the upcoming year. Mind over matter, right?

In the fall of 1992, I chose to join a sorority. The sisters in this circle were supportive and gave me some sense of belonging, and I was content that I could quietly blend into their friendly group. Of course, there were also the constant fraternity and sorority parties or activities for us to be involved in, and I finally managed to make one good and openhearted friend named Renee. She was a huge flirt, very outspoken, bold, and the first openly bisexual woman I had ever met. I could identify with that! She was brave enough to tell anyone who asked and never feared their judgments. We got into tarot cards and spirituality for fun that year, and her personality reminded me a lot of my high school friend Holly's. I was grateful for her friendship, and things seemed to be looking up for me, except I was not happy living at my uncle's and wished I could move. Then, as if by magic, after Christmas, the tenants in my parents' old house on our original homestead gave notice they were leaving. Well, I jumped at the chance to finish out the year in my childhood home and packed up my stuff once again.

The old family homestead had had tenants for the last ten years, and it sadly seemed to lack most of its original charm. The yard was overgrown, the poor house was rundown, and it really felt a lot smaller than I remembered. A friend rented the main-floor bedroom, and I took the south-facing room upstairs. Veronica also moved into the room opposite of mine, and we happily settled in. Everything was good, and it felt comforting to have a home base again. It had been another hard year at school, and I looked forward to being out of classes. I was still struggling with chronic sadness and could not find a way to end the deepening loneliness, even though I was often surrounded by good people. I never felt pretty enough, skinny enough, or bright enough, and it was affecting me on many different levels. "What is wrong with me?" I would wonder and worried endlessly.

My self-esteem was in the bottomless pits, and regretfully at this point I fell into a relationship with a guy, which was emotionally and mentally chaotic. Then, after only four short months of dating, I accidentally ended up pregnant with my first child. Veronica begged me to have an abortion and offered to take me, but I just could not bring myself to consider the procedure. When I told my mom, she was fuming mad and seriously wished I would reconsider. My dad disliked the "baby daddy," but he opened his huge heart anyway and helped us get set up in an old Military base house near them, a couple hours outside of Winnipeg.

Then, after nine long, sad, and sick months, I endured a traumatizing delivery, complete with episiotomy and forceps, which left me even more depressed. Of course, I had not heard anything about mental health in those days, and I just felt horrible. I was struggling with suicidal ideation after emotional upsets, as a way to separate from the pain or rage I was experiencing, and I felt furiously unstable. My son was the only light in this darkness, and thankfully, a good enough reason for me to live at the time. Owen was beautiful, and I loved being his mom, but he never slept very well, and I only managed to nurse him for a few weeks. Of course, I thought he was perfect, but as he got older, we noticed his behaviors became increasingly more peculiar. I did not care or notice too much because I adored him and felt like he gave me purpose. I naively tried to make things work with Owen's dad, but he had his own problems and ultimately, I was forced to split from him after a few miserable years of tears, not getting along, and treating each other poorly.

Seven

ALONG COMES LOVE, AUTISM, AND A THRIVING BUSINESS

In the summer of 1996, I started dating DJ, who had lived next door to me for the past six months and worked for my dad. We had lots in common: we were both Aries who liked to laugh, listen to music, spend time together, work hard, and have fun (birds of a feather). We had undeniable chemistry, and quickly became an inseparable pair. DJ was handsome, tall, blond, and had green eyes and a smile that beamed like sunshine. His humor and strength were infectious, and I loved being in his company. Also, it was sweet that he did not mind that I had a wild two-year-old, and he was kind to both of us. He moved in shortly after we started dating, and we were working for my dad, adulting, and trying to parent, which seemed impossible at times.

My son was getting harder to manage; he was grumpy and battling chronic ear infections, and he even needed tubes put in to remedy the problem. I noticed Owen never seemed to listen to me, his eye contact was lacking, and his twenty perfect words had disappeared around age two. It was beyond baffling. It was then, my mom expressed that she was concerned he might have autism and suggested we have the doctor send him to a specialist. She had raised four girls, and she said, "None were this much work"!

Our pediatrician referred three-year-old Owen for an evaluation with a local clinical child psychologist, and Mom and I took him in. I was extremely nervous, but I could hardly believe my baby might be clinically autistic. It was 1997, and the chances of being diagnosed with autism were 1 in 10,000. Our group was escorted to a gray room that had a child's table in the middle and chairs placed around it. Dr. Macintosh and his assistant had Owen attempt a variety of developmental tests, and they asked us numerous questions about my pregnancy, delivery, family histories, medical conditions, etc. Then, after about twenty minutes, the doctor casually confirmed what I felt was a life sentence for my three-year-old son: he had pervasive development disorder, or PDD-NOS, with autistic type. Oh brother, I was floored, and my mind started to swirl. What had I done so wrong to deserve this? I had taken care of myself, took the prenatal vitamins, and avoided anything that might be bad during pregnancy. How could this happen? Disappointingly armed with a diagnosis, we went home and delivered the sad news to DJ, and he consoled my tears.

With our suspicions confirmed, we quickly qualified for early intervention in helping care for Owen, and we wanted every treatment available to the poor little guy. First thing was for two hours, three days a week in our rural community, an autism specialist named Faye would come practice applied behavioral analysis therapy (ABA therapy) with Owen. I had to set up a blank room with just a carpet on the floor, where Owen and Faye would work uninterrupted with the door locked with an eye and hook latch. Faye would persistently teach Owen puzzles, basic skills, and things he needed to learn, even through his crying and screaming. It was hard to listen to, but she worked magic, and by the end of every session Owen would be mostly calm and maybe even cooperating. Faye was an older woman with a world of experience under her belt, and we were lucky to learn from her. She was fair and firm and reminded me a lot of my maternal grandmother, Grandma Lydia, who had a gift and had dedicated her career to being a principal for children with special needs.

Everything was hard about raising a child with autism at the time, and I remember having to special order books through a local bookstore to study and learn more about his condition. I bought every book I could, though no information seemed promising at the time. Some people argued autism was caused by vaccines, others put their kids on restrictive diets, some parents tried nutritional supplements, reiki, ozone therapy, special detox treatments, exorcisms, as well as any other purchasable "cure" out there. The wealth of information I could gather mostly concluded that autism was not curable, period.

His future looked grave, and I felt sad for him. He would likely never date, get married, have children, graduate from university, or work; we were stuck without a manual for an unmanageable toddler, and that was it. I maintained a great amount of compassion for Owen's struggles and tried to keep up with his wildness, but it was difficult. He would climb up high onto things he should not, empty the cupboards, throw tantrums, chew on electrical cords, play in the toilets, and never liked to play with toys properly. He would line up the items he loved in rows instead. By this point, he had no language, was still in diapers, and had very few useful skills, but somehow, we made it through the days, even if they ended with a few good tears.

In the meantime, DJ and I had been working on a side project with my dad at his farm, and we decided to set our sights on a specialized agribusiness. We took the training courses to start with, bought a twelve-acre farm outside our local farming community, secured major financing, and renovated the old barn. Next, we built a fully furnished lab, got the government permit to operate, signed the exclusive rights to genetics of a major livestock company, and stocked the entire place with merchandise. Then, in September 1998, we opened the doors to our first couple of large customers, with my dear dad being one of them. DJ tended to the work in the barn, while I ran the lab and did the accounting for the business. Everything was new to us, including our very first computer, which I could barely figure out how to turn on. After I mastered that, though, the rest of the computing and accounting came to me quite naturally, and I taught myself QuickBooks with the help of a friend who was a whiz with the program.

This move closer to a small city meant Owen could go to a large daycare center full time and he qualified for speech therapy. These were a huge relief for me, and I was beyond grateful. Faye arranged for a lady who was trained in ABA therapy to practice with him intensively from nine to four, Monday through Friday. This was life changing for Owen, and we felt fortunate to have such a great community and the free governmental supports in place. With Owen being well cared for, DJ and I continued to tackle the wide world of agricultural contacts and went after gaining every new customer we could for our business.

We provided service, product, and training for any farmers new to working with us, and within one year of opening the doors, our little farm became the second most successful liquid genetics provider in Manitoba. I took pleasure in doing the marketing, and DJ was gaining one new substantial farm client every other week. We were happy and hugely motivated by the favorable response from the agricultural community, although it was an intensive and high-pressure job because we were dealing with live product, and the farmers were always on tight deadlines. As such, there was no room for errors without major consequences to the client's farms, and we always had to take the job very seriously.

Besides manufacturing a product that was soaring with posi-tive results, customer service was key in this industry, and we did anything necessary. DJ and I were obsessed with running an efficient and very profitable business, and we loved the many challenges. The opportunity allowed our family to make a sub-stantial living farming and was a life we were both committed to. It certainly was not easy working together, but somehow we navigated our way around the murky waters and made the operation work. In our minds, failure was never an option, and we threw a tremendous amount of attention toward the farm's success. We were young, tenacious, and filled with zest to tackle the life that was unfolding around us. It was insanely busy, but we loved feeling useful and reveled in the blessings life sent our way.

In 2000, DJ and I excitedly decided to marry, with hopes of expanding our family. We planned a small Valentine's Day wedding with only our closest friends and extended relatives and would party the night away like nothing else would ever matter. Veronica was my maid of honor, and our younger two sisters were the candle lighters for the ceremony. We were dressed in our best, and I was wearing a dream gown complete with pink rosette trim and long satin gloves to match. I was ready, but nervous.

A couple hours before the wedding, however, I panicked and quickly phoned the minister to confirm the word "obey" was not in any vows I needed to make. I had witnessed count-less brides promise to obey their husband over the years, and the idea made me nauseous. She reassured me that it was not, and I agreed to move forward with our plans.

While my dad and I were waiting for the wedding music to start before I walked down the aisle, I asked him if he had any wise words to offer the new bride. He looked over, flashed a big, sweet smile, and said, "It's not too late to run." I laughed out loud. My dad was funny this way, but I knew deep down he com-pletely approved of the union. As the night went on, he gave a wonderful speech about writing our own rules for the marriage and wished us the best of luck. My mom also addressed me and DJ with a heartfelt speech and welcomed him into the family. It was a perfect night filled with love, dancing, and people who supported our future, and we were over the moon with delight.

Our plan after getting married was to get pregnant as quickly as possible, because Owen was six already, and he would be starting Grade 1 in the fall. The business was thriving, and it felt like good timing to bring a baby into our lives. After a few months we finally tested positive for pregnancy and were signed up for our newest adventure. DJ and I took the maternity classes, continued to work, went to the prenatal appointments, and prepared to welcome a baby boy in January 2001. I had a wonderful pregnancy, and I felt mentally strong and happy. My mother-in-law came down for the birth, and two days after her own birthday, I went into labor. It was intensive, but with a little help from the laughing gas, I managed to successfully complete a natural birth. Elliot was beautiful, blonde, and such a sweet boy. He was long and chubby, and I loved him the second I saw him. I felt like the luckiest mom and could not wait to get my new baby home. By all appearances, he seemed healthy, and most importantly, to us, neurotypical.

Raising Owen with a diagnosis of autism was still a full-time challenge, and my prayers were answered when Elliot continued to meet his developmental goals and milestones. He had taken to nursing well, and we were securely attached. He was such a smart, silly, and happy baby, and I was even able to teach him some sign language for fun at around eight months old. I mainly spent my days dealing with diapers, laundry, groceries, mealtimes, cleaning, and trying to keep up with house and bookwork. DJ and I were also occupied building a bigger home in town so we could be closer to the school and the daycare that our kids would soon be attending. The house had a nice corner lot, and when Elliot was close to one year old, we moved our belongings into our new home and enjoyed the many comforts it had to offer our little family.

I loved living in the small city, because it helped give me a sense of belonging to a community, and I must admit, I was ecstatic to finally be on the pizza, cable, and internet route! When Elliot was two, he started at the local daycare, because I needed more time to tend to our growing business. Owen was integrated into a life skills program at a nearby school, and we were grateful he no longer had to ride the bus for hours every day. DJ still had to drive out to the farm to work most days, but he did not mind, and we had good staff that he was able to rely on. We were managing dozens of exceptionally large agricultural accounts by this time, and our profits continued to soar.

The clientele were pleased with our services and product and were proudly getting good, consistent results. We regularly catered to our customers with promotional items, freebies, lunches, drinks, and dinners, even if it meant entertaining at our house, and we did it superbly. DJ and I were hospitable and were willing to go out of our way, comfort zone, and often our pocketbook, to gain or retain any farm account. Our livelihood depended on success, so the business really ran our life on many different levels. It was a difficult industry, but we creatively and aggressively tackled it faithfully with passion and vigor. We continued to reinvest our profits back into the farm, land, and inventory and to pay ourselves and our employees well. Owen and Elliot were settled into their weekly routines at school and daycare, and by then I had hopes for one last baby to complete my family. Perhaps a girl?

Eight

PREGNANCIES, THE AFTERMATH, AND DEPRESSION

In early 2004, I had a positive pregnancy test, and we were delighted about the possibility of being parents to a third child. DJ and I adored babies, and I could hardly wait to gestate, birth, and meet our growing little one. Naturally, I waited until the end of the first trimester to announce my baby news, and my entire family was excited and eagerly anticipated the October birth. Everything seemed normal, and I felt good. At eighteen weeks of pregnancy, however, I went in for a routine scan of the baby, and to determine its exact due date. The young woman doing my ultrasound took the required measurements and said she needed to consult with the doctor on call about my results.

I did not really think much until she returned with the doctor, and he had to talk to me about a major problem they were seeing with my baby. He explained the fluid on the back of the fetus's neck was over three times as thick as it should be in that area. It did not make a lot of sense to me, but he said there was a worry it might be caused by two devastating medical conditions. The doctor said I needed to go into the women's health clinic the following week and have an amniocentesis done if I wanted to confirm these findings. I was in total shock, completely confused, and my heart started to swell with sadness. Shit. I went home to deliver the bad news to DJ. He was devastated and we cried and talked, and both agreed that we did not think we could raise another child with complex special needs. Not with the boys we had and the business we had already committed to. We both felt guilty and prayed the scan was wrong. I was afraid but called my mom to deliver the dreaded truth about what we were facing. She listened quietly, and then we both wept for the gravity of the situation.

The day came, and DJ supported me for the appointment. We were escorted into the exam room, and my body was prepped to receive the amniocentesis. The ultrasound technician was present to do the scan and to assist the doctor in drawing the amniotic fluid. Together they did their independent measurements on the baby, and the doctor concluded the fluid was over seven millimeters thick instead of the normal two millimeters. My heart just sank, and I asked if I could at least know the sex of the baby. The technician informed me that he was a beautiful baby boy. *This is pure torture*, I thought, deeply disappointed to choose what happened next. The best medical course of action available to me was a late-term abortion, and the choice felt nearly impossible to make. As DJ and I had decided it was not an option to carry on with the pregnancy, I shamefully consented to a dilation and evacuation (D&E) procedure and was scheduled for the following Tuesday. *God help me, and please forgive me.*

At a full term of twenty weeks, my mom and I made the trip into the city the day before for an appointment to start the process of drying my cervix with a seaweed stick. The doctor explained it was necessary to dilate me for surgery the next day, and that I should be simply fine when it was all over, assuming there were no complications. Of course, I was not going to be okay, but at the time, this was the right decision for my family. Before the operation began, I was prepped and parked in the hospital hallway on a gurney, waiting for this whole nightmare to be over. I was anxious, and furious at God. I felt at his mercy and completely betrayed by him and my body. As I rubbed the sweet boy who wiggled around in my belly, I desperately questioned what he, or I, had done so wrong to deserve any of this. I started to weep at the excruciating sadness that rushed throughout my body, and I literally had no idea how my mind would ever survive doing something so horrific. My heart was incredibly heavy, and I felt as if this was a total breaking moment for me in my life.

Part of the surgery was to use "conscious" sedation, and while it worked at the time to blank out the actual abortion, the horrid flashbacks would slowly start to haunt me for many years to follow. I hated myself and God for making me walk through such a devastating life event, and I was seething mad. I became darkly depressed and had such shame about terminating my pregnancy that I simply told everyone who was not immediate family I had miscarried. The lie quickly made its way through the entire grapevine, and life returned to our normal.

Hope and loving the children we had felt like my only saving graces during these days, but after a few months, DJ and I found out we were pregnant again. It was likely too soon after the abortion, but if it were to be a healthy, full-term pregnancy, we were happy with the idea of being parents for a third time. It was hard, though, because I was still traumatized and anxious, waiting to make it through the first trimester, get an ultrasound, or have genetic testing. The first ten weeks presented as a typical pregnancy, and then one night I miscarried a small gestational sac. I saw my doctor the next day, and he suggested an immediate dilation and curettage (D&C) procedure to remove any leftover tissues or placenta. However, I was not interested in another surgery, and asked him if I could go home and take a wait-and-see approach. It was Friday, and he said if I were not done bleeding by Sunday, Monday would be the day to do the required procedure.

What I did not realize was that my body and uterus would start to aggressively bleed and clot in a desperate attempt to expel the leftover placenta that was still fully attached. Well, that evening I started to bleed profusely, and it would not stop. My friend Renee took me over to the hospital right away, and for the next two hours I lay there as I blurred in and out of consciousness. It was frightening, and the moment I got wheeled into the operating room, I felt like the doctor was saving my life. Of course, I grieved the miscarriage, but mostly I was grateful I had quick access to medical care and that I was going to survive.

I appeared in good health after the ordeal, but my body continued to struggle and feel plagued with chronic pain, sadness, and lingering sickness. Some of these concerns my doctor and I were able to address, but the stuff going on in my mind was whirling and causing me a great deal of unknown distress. My anxieties were through the roof, and my anger and moods were still boiling from my two recent pregnancy failures. Nothing ever felt right, and yet my life looked picture perfect. I had a family who loved me, a great spouse, and two beautiful boys who meant the whole world to me. Yet I struggled and was in total agony, as if I were utterly losing my mind. I spent my time trying to monitor the household environment and organize the chaotic life swirling around me. I was convinced if I could just stay on top of the amazing life that had been given to me, and maybe have one more baby, I would finally feel happy. After all, our farm was still thriving, and we continued to keep ourselves involved with work and raising Owen and Elliot. Logically, I knew there was no basis for me not being of strong mind, so I powered through my days with the same tenacity and obses-siveness that I had always relied on to get me through life's rough patches.

Around this time, we also started to hyperfocus on a new side business, and began pouring our energies into designing, marketing, securing property, financing, and building a large multi-wash facility. It had been a dream of DJ's and it was a practical solution to help us eventually retire from farming. The location picked was perfect, and the services we offered quickly became the go-to place in town. We were proud and could not have been more pleased to watch it grow into a successful venture. It was another feather in our cap, and yet I still felt miserable. I could not figure out what was wrong with me. In fact, my inner critic would often scream those exact words. I had, as loved ones put it, "no reason" to be depressed.

However, in May of 2005, my body and brain physically slammed me into a screaming halt. I had just turned thirty-one, and seemingly out of nowhere, I did not have the strength to get out of bed. A couple days of down time did not bother me, but then it turned into a few more, and by the end of the week, I was no better. I had lost ten pounds because I could only eat a little oatmeal, and I decided to go consult with a physician. Of course, I had searched the internet for my symptoms and had decided it was likely throat cancer because I could not breathe! Truthfully, I had not been able to breathe for ten years, but no doctors ever really listened. One even thought I was plain crazy. So, I went in to see my doctor for his advice. He sensitively and attentively listened to my concerns and then explained that I was suffering from severe depression, likely as a result of the two traumatic failed pregnancies.

Depression? I was not sure about his diagnosis, but I took the prescription for the common antidepressant, filled it, and returned home to the comforts of my bed. As I lay there that night, I kept trying to convince myself maybe the pills could help, but my anxieties were hollering, "That shit will kill you!" The problem was I hated pills because I was sensitive to medications, and I did not like the idea I needed a pill to be happy. I felt like I was dying anyway. *Take the damn pill*, I told myself. I did, and as it made its way into my system over the next few days and weeks, something magical happened, and I began to find humor and hope again in the everyday activities.

I felt better than I had in a long time and wished I had sought pharmaceutical help earlier. As I was contemplating if I should give up trying for another baby, I ended up pregnant one last time, and I was so scared that I had a hard time connecting to my growing belly. I managed to have a textbook pregnancy, but I was nervous the whole time it may not work out. Miraculously, we did get lucky, and after a difficult delivery, we welcomed a baby girl in February of 2006. We named her Belle, and I was totally smitten with her from the first moment I laid eyes on her chubby little cheeks. The labor had been distressing to her, but she was doing well otherwise. I, however, was not.

My hemoglobin levels were ridiculously low, and I was going to need a couple units of blood to recover. I did not like the idea, but I was feeling lightheaded and completely void of energy. So, I consented to the transfusion because my body felt desperate and needed to be replenished. As the two bags ran through my veins, I was astounded at how much better my entire body felt. I spent a couple days recovering in the hospital, and then we got to pack up our sweet little girl and take her home. I could not believe it. After everything my body, mind, and soul had been through, here we sat, blessed with a daughter. Belle was simply beautiful; she had big blue eyes and was born with very dark hair. I was in awe of how sweet and bright she was, and we were so proud of her already. She took to nursing well and reached her developmental milestones right on target. My little family unit was now complete, and I felt euphoric.

Around this time, DJ and I found ourselves with opportunities to invest in a couple large side businesses, and we jumped on the chances. Of course, it was exciting at the time, but they continued to add pressure into our already complicated lives. I imagine most couples would have been drowning in far too much responsibility by this point, but we just kept right on plugging away at the chores. Between the three kids and work, we were more than busy. We loved managing our growing life, and by all appearances we were doing a full-time, excellent job, but it was taking its toll.

DJ and I had spent the previous twelve years so devoted to work and childcare that we had not taken a single holiday. We all enjoyed camping and decided if we invested in a small motorhome, our whole family (and two pet bunnies) could travel affordably and comfortably. DJ loved doing the driving, and this new freedom helped us reconnect with his family who lived four provinces away. These days are by far some of the happiest memories, and it was such fun to travel and entertain ourselves with movies, board games, and delicious snacks. Even Owen was really good on these weeks-long trips up north. We enjoyed being away from the businesses and cherished the time we were able to spend together as a family.

As Owen was maturing into a teenager by this point, his behaviors became increasingly harder to manage, and his pediatrician referred him to a child psychiatrist. He was into head butting, pinching, kicking, and screaming when he could not get what he wanted, especially with teachers and workers who got too close to his face or in his space. We family members would mostly get the pinching and yelling. Once we met with his psychiatric doctor, Owen was prescribed one med for the aggressive behaviors and an antidepressant for its calming effects. The pills worked wonders for Owen, and soon he was back to his happier and more cooperative self. He developed something called macrographia as a result of the medications, but it seemed a small price to pay for the benefits we noticed in his behaviors.

In the fall of the following year, we made one last move into our forever home, and it seemed as if nothing could be better than this. Our businesses were still profitable, and we had comfortably settled into our hectic life. Belle was developing a wonderful little personality, and I adored spending my days with her while the boys were away at school during the weekdays. Every day I would clean, shop, cook, organize everything possible, do laundry, keep the bills paid and the house in order, and get ready for the boys to arrive home at 3:30. I had a fondness for being of service to my family, but it was beyond draining.

My mom friends could relate; I had made a couple good ones over the past years. They were both moms to friends of Elliot, and we became extremely close with the copious amounts of playdates our children required from us. Katie was maybe ten years younger than me, and she was a loud, wild spirit who was hugely outspoken. Quinn was a nurse who was married and at least eight years older than me. She was funny, smart, artistic, and her son was Elliot's best little friend. We had lots of fun with these two families, whether it was going for suppers, movies, to fairs, celebrating holidays and birthdays, having sleepovers, or doing any other activity that was scheduled in town. These ladies were my go-to girls during these days and I adored their company and their children. We supported each other unconditionally and helped with childcare whenever we could. It was a good little network, and the kids were great together.

Then, close to the end of 2008, I felt rundown and went to the doctor for thin, itchy patches on my inner wrists and chest that were not going away. I was not too concerned about it. I had always struggled with sensitive skin, so it did not seem new to me. However, my doctor took a biopsy to determine what was happening, and it came back as extragenital lichen sclerosus, which is a rare autoimmune disorder. "Under a microscope, it looks like shattered glass in the skin," my doctor said. *Of course, I would have this*, I thought, and because it mostly affects the area around the perineum, no wonder I was prone to gynecological sensitivities.

My doctor's advice was giving up nursing to allow my body a chance to heal, and otherwise a topical steroid was the only thing she could offer. Also, she said the condition was likely to flare up around stressful times and I should try to reduce that too. As this was not much of an option, it was more just a reminder to try to look after myself in the midst of our chaotic lives. Belle was to start daycare at this time, and it worked out well to have the extra help with childcare. It meant I could get back to work, as the kids were signed into school and daycare for the day. It was great to have more time to myself, but the truth was, I still felt I could not keep up most days. I was exhausted and often needed an afternoon nap to power through the second shift of my day when the kids would get home.

In 2009, the greatest setback in our career history came to us through a collapse of our primary agricultural markets. We had been at our full capacity that year for animal inventory to keep up with demand, but within a few lousy months the markets were so flooded by over-production that farmers could not give their livestock away. The feed and fuel costs were running high, and many of our large, long-term customers went into receivership or were forced to sell their farms. It was a tough time for us as we watched many of the clients, we had dealt with over the years being forced to close the doors on farms they had loved and had worked so hard for. By some miracle, our farm was still doing okay because we had always been low-cost producers, but the numbers we had once relied on for maximum profits were beyond slacking. Within a year of this collapse, we witnessed a 75 percent drop in our client base, and it was affecting our bottom line.

Of course, there were some government-guaranteed programs in place that could help us pay for general input costs, and we managed to get by this way for a while. In addition, we had to reduce the size of the herd and lay off half our staff because the work just was not there anymore. This was a hard decision, but the numbers had to be working in our favor if we were to continue doing business, and they had long left the building. The only plus to our family was that DJ was more available to us, and this was a pleasant change from the way our life had been insanely running.

On the evening of March 19, 2010, life was good, and our entire family happily celebrated Mom's birthday supper at a fancy restaurant. My sisters and kids were laughing, jokingly having fun, and my dad was sitting across from me. We had started talking about how I felt in a better place emotionally than I had been in a long time, and I attributed it to the low dose antidepressant I was taking. I explained to him how after my late-term abortion I had been in a dark place mentally, and I was finally able to see some "light at the end of the tunnel." It was a wonderful family night, and one that is forever burnt into my memory.

Then, a few weeks later, we delighted in a big family Easter dinner at my mom's house. While seated around the table, my dad started to talk about "believing," because my sisters were saying they were atheist or did not believe in God. My dad wasn't hugely religious, but he knew the Bible and was deeply spiritual, and stated it was, "better to believe in something, rather than nothing. You know, just in case there's any truth to the whole afterlife, or in going to heaven." I thought it was pretty sweet, but I could not have ever imagined he would end up there in a couple short weeks and that our family would be left devastated as a result.

Nine

LOSING MY DEAR DAD, THERAPY, AND PLASTIC SURGERY

My father's death, coincidentally, occurred on the National Day of SAFE Workers. What happened was that while my dad was sliding between a couple rafters needing repair on one of his buildings, he slipped, hit his head, and fell to his death in a split second. My mom had even seen him up there on her way to work and prayed for his safety. She often felt he had this reckless disregard for his life, or an impulsivity to do things he should not, but this time it was costing him his life. The workers in the area frantically watched in horror as he fell thirty feet, and nobody could even stop it. One of the staff quickly ran over to the office and told my mom, "Graham fell."

Mom went running out to see him. The ambulance had been called, and all everybody could do was wait and watch in absolute horror. My mom was in shock, but she strongly sat with him, desperate for help. Her sweetheart was gasping and coughing blood, but there was no cognitive response, and he was dying. Right there on the pavement of his beloved farm. The ambulance pulled up and loaded him in, and my mom was permitted to travel up front. She frantically made her round of calls and then my husband called me to relay the message. I had just left for Winnipeg when the call came in.

"Jill," he said, "your dad has fallen, and it's really bad, like, 'I don't think he'll make it' bad." Shit. I was already heartbroken, and in complete shock.

My sisters, DJ, and I all made our way over to the hospital. As we waited for the ambulance to arrive, we heard an announcement over the PA system that sounded like "Paging Dr. Romeo" to the ER. Lily started crying because she was a fresh nursing student who knew that was the medical term used for a code blue on route. There you had it, and we started to panic. As the medics roared up the platform and ever so quickly wheeled my dad's gurney into the hospital, we could see a medic performing compressions on his jiggly chest.

This felt surreal, and a nurse whisked us off to a family room. She asked if we wanted tea or water. My head was spinning, and just as I was thinking, *what in the hell is going on*, in walks the hospital minister and doctor and I thought, *this cannot be happening*! This was our dad, my mom's husband of forty years, DJ's most trusted friend, my best friend, and my children's grandfather. We loved him, and we needed him, and my kids still needed him. How would I even get through to Owen what had happened to Grandpa? And Elliot and Belle? My mind was flying a million miles a minute, and I wanted to see my dad. I was torn apart because he was going to be alone when he died, and I wanted to be there to comfort him.

Then, in the next instant, our loving nurturer and provider was pronounced deceased, and we were left sadly stunned. The doctor mumbled some things I do not remember and said we could see him to say our goodbyes. This felt impossible, comparatively as bad as my abortion but even worse because my dad had always been a huge emotional support for me, and now he was gone. Permanently gone. No choice, no warning, just absolutely, tragically gone. As we closely huddled around our sweet patriarch, I noticed he looked peaceful. There was a hematoma on his forehead and his leg was broken, but otherwise he looked like himself. We all cried, made quick smalltalk, and then returned home a short while later to tell the kids what had happened.

Owen did not understand, of course, Elliot started to cry, and Belle was only four, but she loved her grandpa, and this made her really sad. Our family spent the next few days trying to comprehend what had happened, accepting dad's death because we had to, and planning a funeral. I had never been good at losing loved ones and losing my dear dad would prove to be no exception.

We hosted a celebration of life ceremony, and over eight hundred guests packed into the United Church we had rented. Old friends, family, farmers, work contacts, staff, and many others came to pay tribute to our dad and to say sorry for our loss. I had written a special letter to place in my dad's casket, and my mom liked it enough to ask if I could read it as part of the ceremony. I was usually awash with fear anytime I had to get up in front of people in the past, but I decided to consent, determined to give my father a proper send off. The backup plan, if I were unable to read, was that Veronica would do it in my place. Miraculously, I mustered up the courage and managed to deliver a lovely speech in honor of our dad, and the rest of the funeral went exactly as planned. The next few days were spent around my mom's house in sadness and shock as we tried to grapple with our family's titanic loss.

My poor mom would have a few different businesses yet to handle, and it was going to require a will of steel on her part. So, it was a good thing she had spent the last number of years learning the ins and outs of the industry and was comfortable making a lot of decisions in my dad's place. They had long ago communicated their final wishes to each other should one of them pass away, and my dad's advice was to "sell it all."

Following the funeral, it was a traumatic time for our family, especially our sweet mom, but she was fierce and brave in the multitude of dealings he had going on with different parties. There were legal matters to settle, farms to sell and clean up, and it was just a difficult situation. Our life mostly went forward in a natural pattern, and eventually life did return to a new normal. It felt like a crushing sadness to Mom and us girls that was almost unmanageable to handle at times, but in our own ways we each coped, grew, and persevered.

I felt devastatingly lonely for the first year without my dad and was prescribed Lorazepam to reduce panic attacks and the generalized anxiety I was experiencing. I found it helped immensely but decided maybe it was time to seek out professional counseling to talk about my hard feelings. I was painfully angry and needed to find a woman who could relate to what was going on with my devastating sadness. I could control everything else, but this I could not control. So, I decided to book an appointment with a female therapist at a healing center, and I was hooked from the very first session. I liked the opportunity to speak with a counselor one-on-one, and I learned a lot from the experience as well.

Cindi's office was warm and receptive. She had cozy chairs, soft lighting, and was a compassionate and empathetic therapist. We had probably six appointments together and were talking a lot about my sexual, physical, emotional, and mental health history, including going back to when I was a child. The truth was, I really did not remember much before the age of seven but had long struggled with sexual impulsivity, and I was desperate to understand why. I needed the misery to end, and Cindi seemed to help. Something I was talking about one afternoon prompted her to gently ask if there had ever been any sexual abuse in my past. I said I did not know; maybe, but I did not remember any details. My mom had told me a neighbor boy wanted to show me his "rubber ducky" once, but I still felt that something bigger had happened with someone else. A shadowy figure, with dark hair and the darkest of eyes, who liked to refer to himself as "Daddy," only it had not been my dad, so it was confusing. I also recalled the smell of cologne, alcohol and cigarette smoke, and a leg-shaped charm that dangled off his thick gold chain.

I admitted I had always had my suspicions before, but I could not tell her any details. Before I left, Cindi casually handed me a printed sex abuse and rape survivors' questionnaire to work on for our next appointment, and away I went. The problem? I was not comfortable filling it out, so I was unable to complete it, and thus never returned to Cindi's office. I figured it was best to leave it at that and get on with life. Of course, I would keep questing for the answers about my younger years of abuse, but I wanted to do it privately, and on my own.

I went home and obsessively researched the topic, and I read it was quite common for survivors not to have conscious memories. Maybe that is why I could not remember the details of abuse? This was tough; maybe I could not do the work because it felt too anxiety provoking and devastating. My soul was stirring, my intuitive nature was in overdrive, and my feelings were dreadfully hurt thinking about the possibility of any childhood abuse. I could not recall anything yet, and I kept busy doing other things in the meantime. Perhaps I would get a quick diploma online for professional organizing? This was more a distraction for myself than anything, but I worked my way through the course and pulled off top marks to graduate in perfectionistic form.

Around this time the shareholders in one of our side businesses made us an offer for our genetic shares that we could not refuse, and we signed on the dotted line to sell. We happily took the money, ran down to the bank with it, and excitedly planned a variety of fun times for our family. I was grateful for the extra security the funds gave us, and as a treat, we bought a few vacations to different hot spots with our children just to make memories and enjoy the oceans. We swam with the dolphins, nurse sharks, and stingrays and did any other adventures we could find.

Still striving for perfection, I also looked into getting more plastic surgery, because I don't know, why not? I had already had a breast lift, and after putting three babies through this wringer, I felt ready for a new tummy. I wanted repair, and it seemed justified at the time to sign up for a full tuck and liposuction. My husband, of course, thought it was completely unnecessary, but there was no stopping my determined mind. I booked the date, had the massive surgery, and woke up feeling like I had been run over by a bus. I panicked, thinking, *what have I done?* The tummy was way too tight, and the stretch marks were mostly gone, but now I bore a scar from hip to hip. This felt like I had lost for winning if you know what I mean. Again, it was one of those decisions I instantly regretted, but the only thing I could do was take the pain prescription and head to the hotel for the night. I lay in a dark room for the next couple days in absolute agony and tried to sleep away the excruciating pain.

DJ tried his best to care for me, but this was too much for both of us. The heavy duty meds were messing with my mind, and I was suffering with horrific nightmares, so I threw them out and opted for T3's. After the doctor cleared me to head home, I thought "Great, I have a nice flat stomach," but the physical and mental pain was traumatizing, and definitely not worth what I had been through. Of course, my poor body would recover in the normal eight-week period, but shit, what a nightmare the healing process had been. I knew I should be happy with the results, but I was still suffering emotionally on too many complex levels.

Ten

PSYCHOSOMATIC THERAPY AND TRAGEDY

Next, as a self-help treatment, I decided to invest in a ten-day course on psychosomatic therapy hoping I could learn more about myself and others. The practitioner was my cousin, and I was hopeful this could be a useful experience for me. I was eager, and eleven other amazing individuals had also signed up. The class worked its way through the lessons in the book, and on day eight we began moving into the more intimate body-work. I partnered with an older woman named Tanya, and we set up our massage table. Our groups followed the instructions on where to find stress in our clients' bodies and how to release the pain being stored in their tissues. Near the end of the day, my cousin said if any of us were holding onto sexual trauma from abuse or rape, she was trained to release that too.

I thought, *I cannot have my cousin do that*, because it required manipulation of the muscles near the perineum area. Tanya quietly asked if I needed the treatment. I whispered I probably did, from stuff that happened to me when I was little—five, maybe? *Where was this coming from?* I thought. Tanya did not want the therapy either, and we decided to decline the offer. We finished the class two days later with a diploma, and I never thought much more about healing any kind of abuse, let alone sex abuse. *People do not actually talk about that, do they?* It did not matter; it was case closed to me. Plus, I could not remember anything, anyway.

Life went on, the kids were growing up fast, and we stayed busy with work and play. It was empowering managing my own little household and business worlds, and yet it was mostly impossible. Owen still had tantrums to deal with, Elliot was a hyperactive child, and poor little Belle sat on the sidelines just trying to take in the behaviors of those around her. After a couple years of grieving the loss of our dear patriarch, my mind had settled into the idea and accepted our new normal. We were spending lots of time with our best couple friends and their children, and we were camping, partying, going out, or hosting dinners: making the best out of life, I guess.

We also planned a trip to the Mayan ruins for Christmas 2012 and invited our best friend Justen and a few of his colleagues for the fun. The big attraction this year was that the world was predicted to end on December 21, 2012. Of course, we did not really believe that, but it seemed like an adventure anyway, plus we would not have to worry about presents this year for the kids. We were all in and enjoyed our trip, including the doomsday at Tulum, which was exciting and historical.

It felt neat to watch large groups of gatherers holding hands in prayer and others walking around with "The End is Near" t-shirts. We even had time for a quick swim in the ocean that day. We also did a day at a caved theme park and celebrated our Christmas there. The weather had been perfect, the food fantastic, and we delightfully finished the trip off in high spirits and returned home to embrace 2013.

This was also the year that we started to seriously question how much longer we could carry on the financial responsibilities of the farm. The governmental support payments were dwindling, and everything was too much work for the monies we were receiving. DJ and I were beyond sick of dealing with the daily demands of our customers. It caused us a great deal of friction because we were perfectionists and wanted to people please, but it was becoming unbearable. We felt stuck and could not seem to decide one way or another on how to call it quits on a business we had started from the ground up. It was our baby, and the cash cow for our family, you know?

Our friend Justen ran a large parcel delivery company, so he could relate to the pressures of running such a detailed service. He was a huge support and a friend we deeply treasured. Justen loved to laugh, hang out, have smokes and drink, and he was a real powerhouse of love and strength for our family. He was a man that we cherished and could not have even imagined life without. But then, as fate would have it, we lost him too. One November night, Justen had a massive heart attack and instantly died on a worksite. His friend frantically called DJ to tell him what happened.

DJ immediately got dressed and dashed to the scene of the tragedy. He watched from afar as his best friend's lifeless body was loaded into the ambulance, and then the reality began to quickly set in. The next few days were spent planning a beautiful ceremony complete with a slideshow and Justen's favorite music. It was a devastating time for everyone who loved him, and it was because of this event we decided to put our genetics company on official notice for the closure of our business. We would stop all production in ninety days, and they could either buy our farm and workable assets or find a new location. We were done.

The owners considered our proposal, and luckily for us, they chose another property. They did, however, buy the inventory and equipment, and thus we got to keep our beloved farm. March 31, 2014 was the day we retired our agricultural business, and at the ages of forty-one and thirty-eight, DJ and I had no idea what we were going to do next. Admittedly, we both felt lost, but we did not much care; the farm was paid for, and we were ecstatic about our newfound freedom!

We stayed busy with cleaning up the farm for the next few months, and I was dabbling in selling a popular diet program. A coach had suggested it to us, and the products seemed to work well for my husband and me. I thought promoting it could not be that bad. However, I quickly learned it was a ridiculous amount of work to run the required info parties, and very few wanted to buy products, if they even bothered to show up. I tried doing the team-building and coaching, but a lot of it was creating excitement about products that were too pricey for most. The company offered a ton of hype, parties, and perks for the people at the top of the sales ladder, but it also created a real frenzied, and manic environment.

As several months went by though, I witnessed a lot of us getting signed up for the business, only to have the money sucked out of our accounts. Honestly, it was the most brutal and failing thing I had ever done, and I hated that. It made me feel like I had been grossly manipulated, and it had even caused a few tumultuous arguments between family members and me. This experience opened my eyes to the wide world of greed and how large operations can prey on the desperate hopes of others. I was mad that I had taken part in the venture, but mostly it was just another distraction. I was still depressed from losing my dad, and still looking for purpose. Who was I? Why was I even here? To suffer?

Eleven

DREAMING THE NORTHERN DREAM

That summer we planned our usual trip up north, but this time a good chunk of the vacation would be spent in Dawson City. Our in-laws were busy mining up there and were having an amazing season finding gold. They had collected a thousand ounces already! Excitedly, we made the forty-hour trip in our motorhome with the kids and two bunnies and camped along the way. This was my favorite, as I always loved having my whole family to myself and making meals and having fun with them or playing board games and crafting. Once we arrived in Dawson, we settled into the Bonanza Campground for the next week. We spent the days hanging out with Grandma Deb, washing gold, and learning how the bars were melted at the gold buyers. We also went to the museum, the fish shack, the

Chinese restaurant, the farmers market, the commissioner's residence, and we watched lots of movies.

Our family has always been a big fan of technology, and we had iPads and laptops available, but by the end of the week we needed a change of scenery. We decided to check into a room right at the campground so our family could spread out for the following week. It was nice to have the full-size bathroom and a big TV. The beds were comfortable, and we were able to spend another seven days making more memories, driving up the Midnight Dome, walking the hundred-year-old wooden side-walks in town, hanging out at Diamond Tooth Gerties, shopping, and picking wild raspberries. It was fun, but by the end of a fortnight, I was stir-crazy and ready to get out of Dodge.

We made the drive back to Whitehorse and spent another couple weeks at our cabin on our family's farm. It was a dreamy, hand-built duplex log cabin with a wraparound deck and a red tin roof. The cabin was set right on the emerald-colored Lewes River and was surrounded by 160 acres of the most luscious forest of spruce and pine trees, deer moss, wild berries, flowers, and bright-pink fireweed. I had not always been comfortable with this place in the wild, but after years of making the trip and falling in love with the land, it felt pretty nice. We often had huge bonfires there with the beautiful fallen wood, while the kids would stay busy climbing on the clay cliffs, fishing, biking, playing video games, or spending time with Grandma Deb.

She was the real reason we would go up north because she was DJ's mom, and he was her only child. His parents had a tough time raising him when he was younger because he was such a wild child, but otherwise, they got along famously. Deb had been a laid-back mom, and DJ respected and loved her.

She had always been warm, welcoming, and full of laughter with us, and I especially appreciated that. We all liked hanging out with her in the woods, and of course, enjoyed her many homemade chocolate cakes. When it was time to head home, there were hugs and tears and promises to see each other soon.

Upon returning home that summer, DJ felt quite strongly this might just be the year to pack some belongings and try a school year up north. He wanted to try living close to his family for a change. I did not know about this. Owen was in his last year of life skills, and I was hoping to see him graduate at least. However, after much thought, debate, and worry, I agreed with the kids and DJ to give it a shot. I was nervous, but we made the essential plans, packed up the truck and trailer, cleaned our house to perfection, and headed out on our journey. Besides, I told myself we could always return home when we had had enough, and that felt like a huge comfort to me.

When we got back to Whitehorse a few days later, we moved into our small cabin and tried to settle in the best we could. It was cramped, but it did not seem too bad at first. Elliot and Belle were signed up for school, and we set Owen up in an old school bus we bought which had been converted into a tiny home. I kept myself busy during the days making the cabin cozy, cooking lots of homemade meals, cleaning, decorating, watching TV, and hanging out with Owen. In the evenings we would burn campfires, split firewood, and sit around chatting. Plus, Deb lived up the driveway from us, so it was nice for the kids to be able to run to her place or for her to come down for supper. The first month was decent, but I could tell Owen was getting annoyed with the numerous power outages up north and was asking for his schoolteachers and friends. *Oh dear*, I thought, *maybe this was not such a good idea.* A common technique for dealing with Owen's meltdowns was to redirect his attention, and this worked for a while, but after another month of not being able to get what he wanted, he started to get more adamant about asking to go home.

We tried to entertain him and keep him happy most of the time, but it was tiring without much support where we were living. I have forever been the type of person to work away my troubles, but I was running myself ragged and my mind was racing and wavering on this adventurous decision. I noticed my anxiety and OCD seemed to be in overdrive, but I felt I was managing, and the kids were having a blast in their new schools. My depression did not seem too bad, but it did not feel good either. My husband was spending a lot of time outdoors processing firewood for fun, and I was beyond lonely. I felt unsettled and could not blame Owen for wanting to go home. I missed my family and friends too.

During this time, our teacher friend Ursula had asked if her and her cousin could rent my house because it was unoccupied anyway. Her condo had finally sold, and she needed a place to live. I trusted her to be there, and if she could pay the monthly bills, that would be great. Of course, this actually happened very quickly, and before I could think clearly about what I had committed to, she had moved in and was loving my home without me. I would get over it, I figured, and our family stayed on the daily tasks of getting the children off to school, building another tiny cabin for Elliot, getting groceries, and doing any other chores we needed to get done. We resided twenty minutes outside of Whitehorse, so getting around was far more work than I was used to. I thought I was doing okay and having fun, but Owen continued to get more agitated, aggressive, and demanding, and it was causing my poor ability to self-regulate to deteriorate.

It was as if I were in a real-life hamster wheel and could not get out. I kept trying to maintain the house, the kids, and my sanity, but getting used to the smaller cabin living quarters was proving to be a huge challenge for me. I felt like I was drowning in my family and pets, and I could not ever get a break from anything. Then our sweet rabbit BunBun died unexpectedly, which I was deeply upset about, and the kids were too. Owen kept barging into the cabin at any hour if he needed help or was upset, and his obsessive and non-stop demands were wearing us all thin; especially me. We tried to make the best of our current circumstances, but Owen's disgruntled attitude was now making me hypersensitive and miserable.

As his mom, I knew darn well this party was likely coming to an end for us, but I just did not know how to pull the pin on our little northern dream. What we had created up there was quite amazing, but after a particularly impossible weekend of battles and outbursts, I finally told DJ he had to drive Owen and me home. I had had it, and Owen had had it. I literally woke up one morning almost throwing up because I was beyond upset, and that was it—unless everyone wanted me back in another depression. DJ agreed to make the three-day trek back home while his mom watched Elliot and Belle, as they wanted to stay there to finish the semester. Without much more thought, I knew we needed to head home. It was a rough few days of winter driving, and then Owen was annoyed because we had left his siblings and our bunny Hoppy behind. Oh brother, we just could not win with him. Whew, my nerves were shot, to say the least.

I phoned Ursula to let her know Owen and I would be returning to Manitoba. I said she could stay in my house for now, but things had not gone well for us up north and our family would need its house back sooner than later. I figured she was set up in the basement anyway, and there was lots of room for all of us. DJ spent one night at home after he dropped Owen and me off, and then with a kiss, away he went. This felt horrible. I had never been away from DJ and the younger children, and I had no clue how this was going to go.

But the next day I went straight to work trying to get Owen re-enlisted in school, and with any luck, hopefully get him a spot in a group-home care facility. He was a large, 6'4" tall twenty-one-year old by this time, and I just could not manage his upsets or pinches any longer. I was worn-out and needed to unburden myself from the pressures of raising a son with autism before I cracked. I spent a few good weeks tirelessly making a case for Owen to live in supported living, but I was not getting anywhere. At last, the school agreed to take him back after Christmas, but otherwise, we were on our own for now.

As I wanted to reunite with DJ and my younger two children for the holidays, I made arrangements with my mom to watch Owen while I was away. Then I shopped, wrapped the presents, packed my bags, and drove into Winnipeg to catch three flights back to Whitehorse to enjoy our first Christmas there. I was glad for the break from Owen, and we had an amazing few weeks without his many upsets. It was a special time, but then I had to make the handful of flights home and did not know when I would see DJ, the kids, and my pet bunny again. What a massive letdown. Upon returning, my only ray of hope was that Owen would be starting back at his high school, and maybe that would make both of us happy. As I figured, he did great and managed to roll right back into the teachers' scheduled ways.

Twelve

THE MAKINGS OF A BREAKDOWN
AND MEMORIES OF ABUSE

I, however, was not doing very well on my own and had been using social media as a way to stay semi-connected to other people. Then one day, out of the blue, I received a message from a school friend asking if I could add a friend of his. He said Meredith was openly gay and battling severe depression. Okay. Of course, I could add her. This seemed harmless enough as we messaged back and forth, until I suggested she come out to where we lived to take advantage of our mental health services. I believed somehow this could save her; I could save her (this was "magical thinking" as she was likely a challenge for the professionals). I was not logically considering the repercussions about what I was saying, but she took me right up on the offer. She needed a ride to where I lived, and for whatever people-pleasing reasons, I agreed. I figured this would be temporary, anyway, until we could find her a place to rent, and it seemed fine. Upon meeting, we became instantly joined at the hip, but she was very dependent, and Ursula quickly grew annoyed with this young woman hanging around the house.

That Friday, I took Meredith to a friend's party, and we were seen hugging, laughing, dancing close, and openly flirting. People were used to this kind of behavior from me, but not while my husband wasn't around. Well, his friend decided to record the interactions and sent the video to DJ. Of course, he was horrified I was acting so poorly, and said "how dare you" share that kind of attention with anyone else?! He was right. I was ashamed, but I was also feeling abandoned by him, out of control, and like there was this gaping void of loneliness or emptiness I could not fill. Plus, I still had no idea when my family was coming home. The truth was, without them I had no idea who I was. Shit, I was a mess, and I decided to fly north again to at least get my children. If DJ needed to be there, so be it, but I wanted my old life at home, with or without him.

Once I got there, we spent the next five days fighting about everything, and then his buddy and video friend were private messaging DJ telling him a variety of bad things about me. Oh man, the whole thing was a gong show, to say the least, and I was spiraling. My feelings were all over the place, and I was desperate for resolve. DJ seemed too scorned to forgive me, and I was deeply upset, but we were hashing things out. Then at one point during an argument he hid my phone on me to get my attention, and I lost it and started trembling with anger. He quickly gave it back, but it was too late, as I was already triggered, and that was it for me. DJ was sorry and agreed I could fly home with the kids. I was relieved for this, because he had originally threatened to keep them from me, but as we boarded the plane, the only thing I could think about was how heart-breaking this whole experience had been on our little family.

Upon returning home to my over-crowded house, I tried to imagine a life without DJ, and him a life without me. I mean, we had been by each other's sides for the last nineteen years and had built a beautiful family life together, and it felt hard to let that go. Plus, he was my best friend, and since my dad had died, my favorite person. After a couple days of sitting alone in Whitehorse and a phone call with my mom led DJ to load up what he could and make the long drive back to us once again. He was still angry, but we could argue about it when he got back. Oh dear, now I had a house full of people he did not like, and it was about to get even more uncomfortable.

Once he arrived home, he assessed and tolerated the situation just long enough to get a handle on it. Then, in DJ style, he put his foot down and demanded the houseguests find elsewhere to live. Nobody else was his problem, and he wanted his family back together. As I felt incapable of fixing this mess of my own making, everyone abided by DJ's stern orders. Meredith went home, and scorned Ursula moved away also. After we parted ways, however, Ursula kept attacking me with hateful texts about what a bad mother and wife I was. At this point, I had had it with her, and in a mad fit, I private messaged her group of friends and spilled the tea on her secrets in retaliation. The note was nasty, and after I sent it, I knew I had stooped to a new low. I had not acted like this since I was a teenager, and it felt terrible. This was not me and trying to keep up with everyone I had recently pissed off was turning into a full-time job. The whole drama felt like a high-school nightmare, and I saw no other way out than to seek counseling again for my outrageous behavior.

As if that were not enough to handle, my sweet Grandma Sophia had died. Plus, Owen finally got a spot in a care home, but only after a three-week stint in our center for adult psychiatry. This had helped stabilize him with the right medications, but it was depressing for me to see him institutionalized and at times in the padded room for poor behavior, as any mother can imagine. While this transition was what our family wanted, I felt like I had failed him and was torn apart by losing my son in my daily life.

Deflated, I went down to our local mental health office and asked to speak to an intake worker. I explained my life felt like an emotional disaster, and that I needed to learn how to sort out my feelings about my current situation and quit fighting with everyone. Marley, the intake nurse, had a one-hour meeting with me, listened attentively while taking notes, and asked lots of questions. I reported experiencing confusion, racy thoughts, anxiousness, and worsening depression, at the very least. My sexuality and loyalties were wavering, and I was worried I might be bi-polar or have Asperger's; or maybe I was just insane, because something was definitely wrong with me. I had always felt that way, like I was bad or defective, and for once in my way-too grueling life, I wanted to get answers. Marley assigned me to a psychiatric nurse counselor named Lina and booked me an appointment with her for the following week. She also informed me that going forward I would have access to the psychiatrist and psychologist based on my individual needs.

Perfect. I felt at rock bottom anyway, so I was open to all the help I could get.

My very first session with Lina was everything I wanted it to be. She even let me give her a hug before we walked into her office, which was super important to me. She was warm, chatty, funny, and reminded me a lot of my long-time friend Paula. There was something comfortable about Lina and how grounded she was in being a woman who helped other women. I instantly felt we were a great match, and I happily met with her one hour a week for the next year and a half and poured my heart and soul out to her. I would go into her office and talk nonstop about my problems and past and the many life events that had harmed me. I relayed I believed there was sexual trauma from childhood. Although I could not quite remember the dirty details, I had determined exactly who the devilish predator had been: my paternal grandpa.

This conclusion was disgusting, deeply saddening, and trau- matic, and I just wished I could remember more. My moods were still erratic, but I kept meeting with my psychiatrist on a regular basis to talk about my traumas and emotional chal- lenges and to adjust my Prozac, if needed. Dr. Lawrence was good with me, like my dad had been, and I appreciated his kindness and encouraging words on whatever recent progress I had been making in the months between our appointments. He made me feel heard and validated, and it was exactly the way I needed therapy to be.

During this time, I also went through a number of psycho- logical evaluations with the psychologist, Carol, to rule out bi-polar, ADHD, or Asperger's. Once the results came back, however, I was unable to figure out what they meant for quite some time. Carol reported I had high anxiety, high OCD, depression, Cluster B traits, a "little bit" of identity disorder because I can dissociate under extreme stress, and what could best be described as "sub-threshold" or autistic symptoms. Carol explained that because I had learned enough valuable skills over the years, I tested as mostly typical. He concluded I needed to keep addressing my childhood sexual trauma to heal the psychological symptoms I was experiencing. As he had already earned my trust, I accepted his diagnosis and continued my counseling with Lina and working on my soul's journey.

In the last month of summer, our family packed our gear and happily made our yearly trip up north. I thought I was feeling well enough to take a break, plus I was armed with a bottle of Lorazepam to cope with anxiety. So off we went to try to enjoy our usual summer camping and activities. DJ mostly kept the kids busy, and I spent my time relaxing, reading, watching movies, and rug hooking. The month seemed like a long commitment, and when I would get irritable, I would go outside to think. My moods were still situationally up and down, and then one day in the silence of the forest, my mind suddenly started to create one crystal clear memory of abuse. I was trapped in the back-leather seat of my grandpa's brown, two-door pimp car in the dark, detached garage, and he was r*ping me. I was watching in horror and trying to scream, but my voice was gone. The abuse felt like punishment for some bad behavior, and he had a lesson to "teach me"—that life hurts—but for me, it was that men hurt if you don't listen!

What I saw made me drop to my knees with heartache, and in that instant, my lifetime of fury towards men was surging through my veins like a deadly poison. This felt like the one puzzle piece I had been missing, and the memory started to ferociously haunt me. These "flashes" would constantly replay in my head to try and process the experience, but it was irreconcilable. I felt destroyed by the realizations and became grievingly sad. No wonder I had been such a mess my whole life! My own grandpa had stolen everything that was safe in my life, and my world had gone dark for decades as a result of his perverse selfishness. Like a thieving wolf in sheep's clothing, he had gotten away with it. My blood was boiling, and I wanted to scream from the rooftops about what a predator I remembered him to be!

Thirteen

DEATH, THE PSYCHIC, DISCLOSURE, AND PSYCHOTHERAPY

Then, at the end of August, just like that, the old bugger died. Warm in his bed, at the ripe age of ninety-two, the grandpa who had once caused me a world of pain was stone-cold dead. My mom called to deliver the news, and she asked if I might like to write him a nice goodbye letter to read for the ceremony, like I had done for my dad. *I would rather die* was my exact thought, but the only words I could get out were, "Mom, he was a pervert, and I am not going to romanticize that!" Shocked, and perhaps not realizing the severity of my claim, she quipped that he had made a pass at her too and at a family friend, Jeni, while at our grandparents' house once upon a time.

That night I wrote my mom a text telling her I was experiencing PTSD-like symptoms from the abuse I was recalling, and I was suffering. Her response? There was not one, and when I heard nothing back by the next morning, I texted her again. I was boiling mad, but she just said that kind of stuff should not be discussed in a text. "Hello? I just broke my silence on sex abuse." It did not matter; she said we should talk about it when I got home, and that was that. I will tell you, I mustered up just enough courage to finish the trip, but it was a difficult issue to bite my tongue on.

When we got back from the Yukon, I had won a free reading from a popular psychic in Winnipeg, and we were curious if my dad would come through. *Please, Dad, I need to hear from you,* was my hope. On September 1, 2015, DJ and I drove to Winnipeg, made our way into the medium's building, and then Keri warmly welcomed us into her office. She said it was okay to record the one-hour session and showed me how to do that on my iPhone. When she started, the first person to come through was my deceased son; he called himself Anderson, maybe Andy for short. He said to tell me that he was watching over Belle and that he would have loved to have played baseball with his dad. He thanked me and said he was protecting me from recent harms, and he knew how sensitive I was. Also, he said he had been by my side as of late.

The next person to come through was my dad. He was with Anderson. She said my dad was warm, had a big smile, and he was out at our farm often. "Enjoy the freedom there" was his message, and she asked if he called me Jillian sometimes. Then she started talking about his accident and said he had had a blow to the head that had knocked him out. She felt he was in medical distress, angina maybe, and panicked to get off the rafter and fell. She felt he was dizzy and had a tightness in his chest. Keri said he was a "great soul, a beautiful, beautiful, man," and I agreed.

I asked Keri to ask my dad what he thought about my grandfather. She said he was terribly angry and that he had no compassion or grace for him. Then I asked if his siblings or any grandchildren had also been affected by his abuse. She communicated my dad said yes and yes. I was stunned, but not surprised. Keri softly asked if my grandfather had been a pedophile, and I communicated that I believed he had been. I said I had been having anxieties and flashbacks, and I was seeing lots of dark images lately about sexual abuse. Keri relayed she believed my grandfather had been an honestly sick pedophile, that he had had a disease of pedophilia and that he could not actually help himself. She said if I started to open up to others, and if I talked about it, I would likely find other survivors. Sadly, I was sure there were.

Keri said she believed my father had experienced the same thing but that he never thought Grandpa had done that to any grandkids. Keri then gave me the message my dad wanted to apologize and say that he was so sorry, and my heart just melted. He relayed about the truth setting me free and that the abuse had happened to multiple people, and that it was generational. I told her I believed so. My memories were of a terrifying man, and Keri explained she believed he was in his own personal hell right now as a result. "Good," I said. Next, she expressed that for as compulsive as my grandpa was, he was really, really smart and did things when kids were very small until we would get old enough to tell. That was exactly what I had suspected, and I admitted I was sure I had been groomed since day one. I said most of the abuse had happened, and ended, at age seven, just before my eighth birthday.

Then she said, "Your soft-hearted grandma knew, but she never knew what to do about it."

I stated, "I'm sure she did," because I thought I had told her he hurt me during the week of the abuse. Keri expressed Grandma was now protecting the family, and if she could do life over again, she would have left him. She was trying to make up for the generational consequences of her choices. Also, Keri said my grandma and dad were together and they were expressing that I should be teaching and to continue to work through my feelings. Keri then suggested I learn the Emotional Freedom Technique and said she thought it could help release trauma stored in my body. With that being the end of the hour, we hugged, said our goodbyes and thank yous, and walked out feeling completely floored by the reading. I felt validated by my dad and confident I needed to try and talk to my mom about this again.

For the next week I seethed and tried desperately to remember what else I had forgotten. I woke up every morning at 6:00 a.m. and pulled a scribbler out to jot down anything I could put together about the memories of abuse. I made lists of things I remembered hearing and seeing, my endless triggers, my impulsiveness and flirtatious sexuality, my sexual history, symptoms of abuse, past clues, reckless behaviors towards self or others, and any other details I could piece together.

During this time, it was like the floodgates had broken open on my memories, and I felt emotionally and mentally broken and still desperately in need of eradicating this pain. I found myself filled with a red-hot fury for answers, and I obsessively researched dozens of articles on incest or abuse and found a life-changing book titled *Secret Survivors: Uncovering Incest and Its Aftereffects in Women* by E. Sue Blume Wiley. Inside its pages lay a wealth of wisdom and her original questionnaire for incest survivors, which I filled out and scored a 16/16. Well, I furiously chose to get brave and arranged for my mom to come out to our farm so we could talk about my reading with Keri, plus the nine full pages of notes I had been working on and my stack of articles on surviving childhood sexual abuse.

She listened to the recording but wanted nothing to do with my notebook, and she quickly slid it back in my direction. "Okay, so what did he really do then?" my mother brazenly asked. Well, I quickly died, to say the least, and courageously voiced the three main abuses that no mother would ever want to hear out of a daughter's mouth. Next, I asked her if Dad had ever mentioned any sexual abuse because I remembered Lily once telling me he thought maybe his dad used to abuse him. She said, "Never." Okay, well, my news was shocking and uncomfortable, but I promised her I would keep my stories to myself for now. Mom told me she was glad I was getting help, gave me a hug, and went back to her day. It had gone fine, I supposed, and I felt mostly relieved. I was glad I had given voice to the abuses and broken my silence to my mom, but I was also sorry it had taken me decades.

I continued to go to therapy every week, worked through my emotional ups and downs, and faithfully took my antidepressant. I also finally took my husband's last name after fifteen years of marriage, as I no longer wanted to bear any connection to my grandfather's surname. DJ sweetly welcomed me to the family, and I had a new name to be proud of. Then, around Christmas

2015, my mom and I were having a conversation about what rebellious teenagers us girls had been. Admittedly, she could not figure out why my teens were not like that, because my kids were so good. Then I piped up maybe it was because they had not grown up with a perverted grandfather. She glanced at me with skepticism and said, "I just don't see how." Well, as I could not explain the full story to her or myself yet, I immediately dropped the conversation to avoid confrontation.

I went home stunned she did not seem to believe me and was working through the hard feelings for months because this was tough to reconcile. Then, at the end of one of my therapy sessions, Lina announced to me that she was retiring. Of course, I was happy for her, but I dreaded the idea of starting with a new psychiatric nurse. Lina said the woman replacing her was one of two nurses and both were fabulous. I trusted her opinion, so I gave her a big hug and told her to have a wonderful retirement. She wished me the best of luck and said I could expect a call about an appointment with a new counselor soon.

After about a month, though, I still had not heard anything back from Mental Health about any upcoming appointments. I was not doing well without the emotional support, and my moods were getting the best of me every day. DJ and I were still arguing over past issues, and everything anyone said seemed to be triggering me into a fury, or hopelessness. Plus, I was sleeping a lot because I felt beyond miserable over having no one to work through my struggles with. Thankfully, a nurse named Lindy called and said she could see me later in the week to help me get back on track!

Our meetings would take place in the same office and building, so I was happy about this. Lindy was dark-haired, friendly, smart, and intuitive, and I immediately knew we were going to be a good fit. Her energy reminded me of my dad, and it felt comfortably familiar. We continued with months of psychotherapy appointments and went through my history, what had brought me into therapy, and my emotional problems with interpersonal relationships. We talked about retiring our farm, trying to live in the Yukon, and my breakdown, and I told her putting Owen into supported care had been extremely hard, and that I missed him.

I talked about my rage at the abuse and just never feeling "okay." I felt chronically shell-shocked and traumatized by the memories I was experiencing, and Lindy recommended Dialectical Behavior Therapy. Lina and Carol had previously mentioned it to me, but it sounded like more work than I could handle and seemed like too big a commitment. It involved me going to outpatient classes at the Adult Psychiatric Centre one day a week for two hours. The sticking point for me was that it was a six-month course. Six months of school, homework, and behavioral modification? I did not know about this, and the commitment worried me. Lindy cleverly encouraged me to put my name on the list and said I could opt out if I was not ready when they called. *Okay, fair enough*, I thought. I continued to see Lindy for the time being, and to manage the life swirling around me all while trying to heal from the atrocities of my still silenced and vicious memories. It was incredibly painful, and I was keeping to myself a lot to try to soothe the suffering I was experiencing.

During these months, I stayed busy reading every helpful book I could, which even included studying relevant parts of the DSM-5 published by the American Psychiatric Society.

My book and audiobook libraries included: *The Female Brain,*
Rising Strong, I Hate You-Don't Leave Me, Overcoming Perfectionism,
Odd Girl Out, Complex PTSD, Rage Becomes Her, Healing the Wounded
Heart, The Truth, The Science of Evil, Daring Greatly, The Book of
Joy, Waking the Tiger, The Art of Living, Out Came the Sun, The Body
Keeps the Score, Getting Past Your Past, and I Know Why the Caged Bird
Sings. I studied these books as research, and I decided to start
quilting again for fun after a twenty-year hiatus. This proved
therapeutic, and I was mostly sewing baby quilts for my beloved
new nieces and nephews. I picked only the brightest children's
patterns and made as many block and rag quilts as a girl could.
I was doing fairly well, and then after Christmas, Lindy notified
me that I had been accepted into the Dialectical Behavioral
Therapy program starting in the spring. I weighed the benefits
and thought: *Maybe I am ready to do this*!

Fourteen

DBT THERAPY AND A WEDDING BARN?

The free course would run from March 2017 through until the end of August. Class was scheduled for Wednesday nights from six to eight, and if we completed it, we would get a certificate and a key chain with dialectical behavioral therapy notes on it. The psychologist was a small, older woman named Dr. Kathryn, and she welcomed twelve ladies into the Wise Minds group on our first night. We started with our introductions, did a short-guided imagery meditation, and then got right to work learning the lessons in the thick manual for DBT. The teacher was sensitive and amazing, and the other women were from many walks of life. Some were suffering from alcoholism, abusive relationships, BPD, bipolar, ADHD, or were there on Child and Family Services orders, but notedly, what we all had in common, (besides blue eyes), was emotional dysregulation.

These ladies were going to be my group for the next six months, and I was stoked for the process. I committed myself to healing and decided I would not miss one class if at all possible. I was hooked on the therapy, and for the first time in my life, I sat at the table with vulnerability and passion. During the lessons we were encouraged to discuss our feelings, triggering events, and any other family issues that were affecting our abilities to cope. We also talked about what we were actively doing to try and correct behaviors that were getting in our way of healthier functioning. One hard part for me, though, was I would get ridiculously anxious about speaking up when it was my turn. However, Dr. Kathryn had a gift with her caring interactions, and she made me feel heard and supported when it was my turn to talk, and this was incredibly helpful for me. She was warm, attentive while listening, and would always close our conversations with the phrase, "Thank you for sharing."

Dr. Kathryn was smart and insightful, but most of the women could not manage to follow through with the commitment, and thus abruptly stopped showing up. The rule was, if you missed more than three classes without good reason, you were put back on a waiting list, and the spots were filled with new recruits. Over the next few months, we shared our stories with each other, as well as our behavioral struggles, and collectively offered support wherever we could. I allowed myself to get close to a few of the women on a reasonable level, but I had to work hard on boundary setting so as not to be engulfed by their troubles, as I had been prone to do this in the past. This time it was about me, and that was my only focus. I went to every class except for one, and six short months later, I earned my certificate for working through the Dialectical Behavioral

Therapy course. I was proud of this success and decided it was time to get working on something a little more fun. Maybe another project DJ and I could do together?

After a ton of brainstorming and researching the internet, I decided the next thing I would like to try career wise would be a wedding barn. DJ and I had always excelled in customer service and sales, and we figured this could be an opportunity to showcase our beloved farm. It was going to take time to gut the buildings and renovate, but we were up for the challenge and came up with a plan. I drew up notes and sketches, printed stacks of resources, figured out ideas for the place, built a website, and invested in some wedding decor. We also renamed our farm Apple Acres to better reflect our new organic lifestyle. In an effort to fund this new project, DJ had contacted Ducks Unlimited to apply for a watershed grant that would lease 147 acres of wetlands from us, and once it was accepted, we went straight to work.

We started by taking our equipment apart, stripped the barn, made trips to the dump, burnt everything else we could, and renovated the facility to perfection. It was complete with white tin, four beautiful sets of glass patio doors, a modernized bridal suite, a bar, and a brand-new cement dance floor. I deco-rated the whole place as cute as could be with props and took lots of photos, while working on a liquor license. Everything was turning out wonderfully, and I had even booked my first bride for 2018. This was exciting, but the Liquor Commission required an engineered blueprint for the wedding barn. Well, without much worry we hired a local engineer to approve the building and carried on with our plans. However, when his report came back, it was determined that the rafters were "failed." We had had lots of snow that winter and a bit of leaking in the barn, but it had caused enough damage to make the place dangerous.

I was stunned and now had to deliver the news to the bride less than three months before her wedding. The solution I offered to her was that if she could find a wedding tent to rent, we would offer the location free of charge to help make her wedding happen. Thankfully, they found a tent, and the bride was even cool about losing out on the barn. Mostly, she loved the property and was happy to be able to make the best of the park-like space. Her groom arrived in a red helicopter, the weather cooperated for the ceremony, the catering was exceptional, and the invited guests merrily partied the night away. The wedding was a grand success, and we were grateful to have pulled it off. It had gone well except for a couple missing things and a mess, but it also made us decide maybe this was too much. Tolerating droves of party stompers on our acreage seemed like a business we would steer clear of in the future. It had been fun, but once this wedding had passed, I took down our website for services and finished up with the wedding barn dreams. With that out of the way, I started the fall feeling fairly good, but was hugely struggling with PMS, of all things.

I was still in bi-weekly therapy with Lindy at this point, and she suggested talking to my psychiatrist about my monthly moods. He made a slight increase to my antidepressant, and we continued our appointments. The headlines dominating the news around this time were reports of Harvey Weinstein's grotesque abuses of power and his predatory rapes of women in the movie industry. Coined "The Weinstein Effect," the world heard dozens of Hollywood beauties, actors we admired, come forward and publicly admit that this revolting man had attacked them. Their #TimesUp claims enraged me, but I was also so proud of the clan of powerful women who bravely spoke up against his injustices. Rose McGowan's "Name it, shame it, and call it out!" statement really hit home with me, and it fueled my fire even further for seeking my own justice.

The #MeToo stories everywhere were stirring up a ton of tough emotions for me, and then the Dr. Nassar scandal broke, and I was even more mortified. He was an old man who had abused his power like my paternal grandfather; a pervert who got off on hurting girls right under the noses of their mothers. I watched in agony as this magnificent group of young women faced the world and their once-trusted coach to bravely recount their painful tales in a globally televised reading of the survivor-impact statements at the end of his trial. Wow! This made me sick as a mother of a precious teenage daughter and as a girl who had been affected by a calculated predator. Yet, I fully celebrated these beautiful young women for breaking their dark silence and wished I had been able to do the same so long ago. What a difference it could have made in my life!

Fifteen

"LET THE RECORD SHOW"

Maybe I was ready to speak about the flashes that had been whirling around in my mind for the past three years. Where would I even start, though? I tried to process and organize the memories of abuse and was working on negating the effects it had on my mind, body, and soul. The truth was, I had felt in traumatic pain ever since age seven, and everything I had been experiencing now made perfect sense to me. Everything: my lifelong depressive attitude, my weak immune system, my miscarriages, my distain for authority, my attraction to dominant men, my tremendous fears, troubles with emotional regulation and interpersonal relationships, and my total absence of self-worth.

It was sad to realize and accept such an unfathomable truth, and I counted on my counseling with Lindy to work out my angers. She was great, but I soon realized I was going to have to speak about the dirty details of the memories that haunted me in order to heal them. At this point, I was forty-three, and even though it is completely safe to tell someone, I realized it was going to be hard to connect to the words that would need to roll off my tongue. After all, they had been trapped in my throat, mind, and body for the last thirty-six years!

On December 18, 2017, I decided the secrecy pact I had once been coerced to take had to be defied and that acknowledging the experiences was my "proof" the abuses had in fact occurred. As my young child's mind never wanted to believe my grandpa would abuse me, it had split me into a frequency where fantasy was always preferred over reality and where silence and perversion seemed to fester. It was here in this darkness where I had struggled with situational, delusional, and irrational thinking over the years. I trusted Lindy, though, and told her that thanks to DBT therapy, eye-movement desensitization reprocessing self-help therapies by Francine Shapiro, and studying my collection of favorite books, including *Rising Strong* by Brené Brown, I was ready to open up about my story. I was nervous, but I bravely figured it was a now or never kind of session, and I needed to give voice to what I had remembered.

For this important appointment, I rolled up my sleeves, got comfy in my chair, and began methodically describing the tragic ways in which my fifty-pound body had been trespassed against so many years ago. I recounted in detail fourteen predatory rapes that I believed occurred the week my parents vacationed and hand-drew where and how each one happened. I also told Lindy there were six other similar sexual assaults from slightly younger years, including one that was particularly traumatic to talk about. I explained how he had gotten away with it was, that after everyone went to sleep, he would sneak into the guest room, lock the door, and then act out whatever piggish fantasies he wanted, early in the morning and late at night.

After a few days, he ramped up the endless "games" and he would sneak us out to one of the garages or to the downstairs bathroom to play. He called those delusional acts natural and loving. I now know to confidently call them rape. However, at the age of seven, I had no clue; I just knew I hated it. Plus, I was delirious from lack of sleep and could not tell if these were just nightmares I was experiencing at the time. During the abuse, if I protested, he would say I was gay, going to hell, or that I was sinful, and nobody would ever love me. If I tried to scream, he would silence me with a heavy hand, and if I would cry, he would laugh, but if I was bad, I would be choked, have my cheeks pinched, be tickled hard, have my arm twisted, wrists squeezed, or was otherwise hurt.

I had survived by dissociating from the torture at the time, and then had to try to piece together the fragmented memories for decades to follow. My grandpa had threatened me, and anyone I loved was also fair game should I ever tell anyone about our little secret. He had justified the abuse by calling it love or by saying that I needed to learn discipline, because Grandpa was a firm believer in the phrase, "Spare the rod, spoil the child." As awful as the abuse itself were the names he called me, and the way he swore at me when he got angry was intimidating, demoralizing, and filthy. My grandfather was a skilled predator, and he used every trick in the book to groom, sexualize, and silence me to his perfection. It had worked, and I had paid the price, serving a lifetime in misery for his crimes! I was furious about his narcissistic and psychopathological behaviors, but I also felt good about the disclosures and newly empowered.

At last, I had proudly spoken up for my seven-year-old self, because I knew the girl inside me had suffered in a dark silence for far too long. As our hour came to a close, Lindy asked if I was going to be okay when I went home, because it had been such an intense appointment. I let out a big sigh and said I was relieved.

"If I died tomorrow, at least one person knows the truth, and that means the absolute world to me," were my exact words. After three years of extensive psychotherapy, the lid had blown open on the disgraceful secrets that had bred nothing but a grotesque shame and shackled me in a personal hell for most of my life. I thanked Lindy for being incredibly empathetic, for holding sacred space for me while I engaged my trauma, and for truly helping me. When the appointment ended, I went home stressing with sweat, but optimistically looked forward to 2018, as the energy now felt officially cleared for my future self to grow.

I continued to attend counseling every two weeks, and that spring the repairs to our barn roof started, and the farm was again buzzing with activity. This was the way we liked it. Summer was always fun, as we did a massive garden and a ton of landscaping, burning, and clearing out of any old clutter. The months went by fast and soon enough DJ and I and the kids were back to the grind of school in the fall.

Sixteen

"THE SPARKS OF SPEAKING
TRUTH TO POWER"

I have always been a huge political buff, and what was swirling in the news during September 2018 was the jaw-dropping live testimony of Dr. Christine Blasey Ford against Brent Kavanaugh. I watched this breaking story and sat completely glued to her emotional testimony, in front of the world, against her alleged attackers. It was enraging, and I felt horrified by every single detail of her scary encounter that she shared with the world. As she professionally stood against the US Republican's apparent "firing squad" who tried to minimize her claims, it sorely reminded me of the Anita Hill trial I had watched in 1991. Although this time there were compassionate efforts made by the democratic leaders to help support Christine with their comments or questions. She was there on behalf of every woman who had never spoken up, and I proudly backed her public efforts to change the dialogue about speaking up against all sexual assaults.

Women across North America were collectively empowered too and spontaneously started reporting their rapes, and the movement swept the country like wildfire. It is an impressive fact that RAINN, the Rape, Abuse & Incest National Network, saw an influx of calls up by 147% the day Dr. Ford took the stand against her perpetrators! Dr. Christine Blasey Ford is a hero in my book, and her testimony got me thinking about furthering my journey towards speaking up no matter the feared consequences.

Lindy was very pregnant by December of 2018. We had a few more sessions together, and I was excited for her new baby but now had to face the reality of another new counselor. On my last appointment I brought Lindy in a card, wished her the best, and thanked her for everything she had done for me. She had cracked open my secrets, and I would always be grateful to her for that. Lindy assured me her replacement would be very good, and I looked forward to meeting her. Lara was the psychiatric nurse assigned to handle my case, and she was a bright and inquisitive woman who took notes on everything I said. She was relatable, smart, and caring. I was seeing her every three or four weeks and talking about life events that had been triggering me, trying to figure out how to work on them. I was mostly just venting about them, which helped, and I was doing well otherwise and settling into 2019.

Then in March, HBO aired the documentary called *Leaving Neverland*, and I felt obligated to watch it. MJ had been a musical favorite of mine growing up, and I was curious to hear the personal stories from the men who had survived his abuse when they were boys. I watched the four-hour, two-part series and I regretfully related to many of the boys' experiences. I empathized deeply with their lifelong pain, and I kept thinking, *selfish, sick, predator.* I believed Wade Robson and James Safechuck's timeline of events, and then I watched, "Oprah Winfrey Presents: After Neverland."

As the show started, Oprah said, "This moment transcends Michael Jackson; it is much bigger than any one person. It is a moment in time that allows us to see this societal corruption; it's like a scourge on humanity. It's happening in families; we know it's happening in churches and schools and sports teams everywhere." I jumped out of my seat in praise of the words that had just been spoken, and completely agreed with the phrase, "Bigger than any one person!" It was brilliant, and out of the mouth of such a wise and respected woman who had once been a friend to the now-disgraced pop star. *AHA!mazing* is all I could think, and I was in proud support of Oprah's efforts to once again bring forth the bravery required to speak against child sexual seduction and abuse.

After the program aired, I asked my mom and sisters in a chat if they had watched *Leaving Neverland*. Lily and mom had, and mom admitted she had learned a lot about how seductive the predators can be. She said asking your kids is not good enough, that children will lie to protect someone they love. I agreed and said, "their mother from the truth." She replied, "Yeah."

The following week, I accidentally stumbled across another HBO movie that was based on the true story of Jennifer Fox, a successful woman who had to return home to remember her past. Her mother had found a concerning story in her old room, titled, "The Tale" about a "special" love between Jenny and her childhood horse-riding coaches. Looking back at the nature of the relationships, which had turned sexual, Jenny realized she was thirteen and that she had told herself it was love in order to survive the truth about the abuse. The movie was incredibly empowering for me, and I felt honored to know her story. My favorite part was the end of the film, where Jenny confronted her abuser in public. I jumped out of my seat and cheered for her character like I was at a sports event! It was a true moment of taking back her power and acknowledging that what had happened to her was wrong on every level.

After watching these programs on childhood sexual abuse, I became extra sad, and fell into quite a grieving for the next few months. It was also during this time that I started studying BPD and was questioning whether I had it. I definitely fit the criteria, and I asked my psychiatric nurse about my official diagnosis. It read "deferred," but Lara quickly scanned her computer files and casually confirmed that yes, based on the notes, I did have BPD but was "successfully treated." I had seen my psychiatrist write down "histrionic" before but had not pieced together that my Cluster B traits were the borderline criteria, and I was surprised by the news. This, plus the realization about my own past and the rage at the unaddressed sexual traumas that had happened to my younger self, were mind-bending. As I went through my countless memories and grieved for what had been stolen from me, I began to see very clearly how deeply the abuse had affected my behavior my entire life. From my base of underdeveloped or perverted thought patterns, I was often trying to recreate abuse, hurt others, or self-harm in mild forms, at times blowing up my life with extreme choices.

A lot of my obsessions were strong over the years, and the urge to resist felt impossible at times. I often felt out of control and wanted to dominate others as a form of controlling my environment. I had also created a fantasy script since Grade 3, believing that if a boy "loved" me, I would be relieved of my life-long loneliness. As a result of this, I was a huge flirt with everyone over the years, without any regard for other women's feelings, and I took whatever I wanted from men, even if it was just attention. I realized I had been insensitive to other people's pain my whole life because I had been drowning in my own misery of unspoken pain. One family bully had caused it, and I had spent decades punishing everyone I came in contact with because of his abuse. Now I understood where my mountain of bottled-up rage had stemmed from, and I felt it was time to use my story to help anyone who might be experiencing abuse or who had already survived the horrors, so I started furiously writing this book. As I was never educated on sexual abuse or how to disclose what had happened to me, and I did not want others to spend decades driving themselves crazy in a dark silence of shame and denial!

I spent the summer of 2019 maintaining our large garden, cutting grass, enjoying the Manitoba heat with family, and taking a break from writing, but news about childhood sexual abuse was always of interest to me. As such, I had been following the details of convicted pedophile Jeffrey Epstein's disgusting behavior of running an underage sex-trafficking ring. The press was releasing one story after another, and the particulars about the disgraced financier were infuriating. They were hurtful to hear as a survivor, and as the very protective mother of a beautiful thirteen-year-old daughter, I was beyond horrified.

Being the coward Epstein was, authorities reported he took his own life in his prison cell on August 10, and I honestly felt relieved that this perpetrator had been removed from the planet. Of course, there has been much speculation that his death was murder, but either way, I am satisfied that he cannot hurt any more girls. The women who wanted to speak against him have had that chance nullified, but together they are working on suing his $577 million-dollar estate and bringing his madams to justice. Ghislaine Maxwell is an abhorrent pervert for allegedly helping procure young girls for Epstein and company's consumption, and she will hopefully pay dearly for her crimes, if they can successfully prosecute her. I stand behind Jeffrey Epstein's bold survivors and wish them enormous success against the betrayals of every perpetrator who delighted in harming them as girls. I also wish the group healing and I wish them all love. ❤

Seventeen

THE BODY STORES TRAUMA

Through reading my story or others' stories, you might be able to imagine that the pain of childhood sexual trauma does not just go away. You don't "get over it," you can't deny it away, pray it away, drink it away, "f*ck it" away, or banish the physical, emotional, sexual, mental, spiritual, psychosomatic, and psychological damage that has occurred within your body. The trauma happened, and your body remembers!

Physically, over the years I have suffered with: fatigue, asthma, ear/nose/throat problems with related surgeries, headaches, irregular periods, miscarriages, and allergies or sensitivities to: stress, florescent lights, latex, sulpha drugs, peanuts, tree nuts, sesame, smoke, candida, dust, mold and environmental allergies, perfumes and chemicals, most metals except titanium and platinum, excessive heat or cold (makes me itchy), cold meds, psyllium, pine, newspaper and magazines, sulphur-based foods, poison ivy, eucalyptus, wool, alcohol, sulfites, food preservatives, rough fabrics, and too-tight clothes with tags. Yes, basically, I have been completely uncomfortable forever and have exhausted all resources trying to identify my life's irritants. I have done every natural treatment available, such as: acupuncture, massage therapy, diet, vitamins, allergy testing, exercise, yoga, intravenous ozone, colonics, candling, cupping, you name it, and while these can each be helpful, they are not a substitute to seeing licensed, well-qualified mental-health professionals or a doctor if you are having unmanageable symptoms leftover from incest abuse.

Bless those who believe otherwise, but in my personal experience, alternative therapies alone did not work for the complexities of my condition. I needed medication and psychotherapy. I also had to turn down my stress, learn to hobby, stretch my body, eat healthier, use DBT skills to manage my relationships, mindfully practice kindness, and even adopted a handful of cats for emotional well-being. These have all helped turn down the mental anguish I felt for decades, and I am forever grateful for the interventions.

When I was breaking down in 2015, my psychiatrist prescribed Fluoxetine as an antidepressant, and this drug has been an important part of my daily routine for the last five years because it helped tear the veil off my lifelong delusions. I cannot say how, but it really cleared a lot of my mental confusion and helps keep me happy. It has been a game changer in my mental health, has improved my focus, and it helps me not feel so physically stressed or irritated by those around me. Please work with a good doctor to find medication that is right for you.

Emotionally, I have struggled my whole life to regulate my feelings because my child-like temper often gets the best of me and has had me in hot water more times than I can possibly remember. I would equate my emotions to a pendulum, except there was no middle ground; just the black or white of raging or satisfaction. I could never successfully communicate why I was angry and prone to quick tears or rage. In the past, I often defied people's well-intentioned advice to get what I wanted, and I did not care if it caused rifts between me and those I was closest to. For years, my moods would go up and down on a daily basis, for any number of reasons, and I had no control over the torment. It was the highest of highs when I was happy, or the darkest of lows when in crisis.

When I was angry at someone, I would want them dead, and if I were sad or mad, I would wish myself the same demise. The abuse had long ago annihilated my core self, and for decades I was desperate to find anything to medicate the painful void that it had left behind. I have been emotionally over-reactive, and in cases have caused harm to myself and hurt others' feelings before gaining experience in DBT therapy on how to best regulate myself in difficult situations. However, my physical symptoms can still be strong at times; when anxiety hits, I feel deep dread, the need to escape, like the room is closing in and it is hard to breathe. When I feel extreme anger, it can seem like a bomb goes off in my chest, and my mind gets really racy. Loneliness or feeling abandoned used to be, or can be, the worst, and in these cases work, love/sex, distraction, comfort food, or music, have often been my drugs of choice.

Sexually, I have been a beautiful mess, and often reckless with hearts, because of the abuse I endured. Being womanized at the age of seven by my fifty-seven-year old grandfather under the guise of "pretend, practice, fun, obedience training, or romantic love," followed by threats should I ever tell anyone, completely affected me. As I was exposed to severe, repeated sexual traumas to my entire body that were way too terrifying to deal with at such a young age, my mind defensively denied they ever happened.

This shame I experienced was so blinding I selectively silenced it for decades, and the truth was that my grandpa had totally harmed my feminine nature and had annihilated my self-esteem in doing so. I hid the damage well, but it has always been under the boiling surface of my hypersexual personality. When I was young, it seemed easy enough to hide my desires, but they were there, especially when I had sleepovers with girlfriends, crushed on cute boys, or watched romantic scenes on television.

I chose to start having sex at age sixteen because after nine months of dating, it seemed like the thing to do. Well, I took charge of the whole first encounter like a pro, only to have it end awkwardly with the boyfriend asking, "Are you sure you haven't done this before?" (because I knew what to do and hadn't bled), to which my answer was a quick, "Nope." I was quite shy about the curvy appearance of my body during these years, but never of how I could use it to get what I wanted, especially out of men.

Men had long been attracted to my plump lips, playful nature, curly brown hair, and blue eyes, and my love for flirting would catch their many interests. I loved attention, and I was always chasing after my latest crush, almost obsessively, but usually after I slept with a boyfriend, I would want to dump him—especially if the sex was a bad experience, which it often was. I found everything about it to be too much or wrong, and I would be left feeling ashamed or completely disappointed.

My husband, DJ, however, has been good about my open sexual nature, preferences, dislikes, and need to feel in control, so we have been fortunate that way. The rare times my sexuality has been a problem in our marriage is when I have kept loose boundaries in friendships, and it has only created jealousy or hurt feelings amongst those involved. So, what I have learned about hearts is that few who signs up for a true marriage of monogamy wants any kind of third party. I understand a lot of people like the idea of "openness," but my husband signed up for one sweetheart, and that alone works for us. (I would invite you to read Neil Strauss' book, *The Truth: An Uncomfortable Book About Relationships*, should you need a good reason to whole-heartedly commit to one person.)

Spiritually, I had been questing my whole life to figure out who I was, what my purpose was, and why I was so chronically miserable. When I was younger, I relied heavily on God, prayer, and magical thinking to find a little solace because that is what I had been taught growing up. It was only when I got to university and started studying different religions I realized there were countless ways to fill your soul. Buddhism was attractive to me, and I enjoyed its simplicity, but at the time I felt spiritually empty, perhaps even dead. For years, prayer remained the only tool in my box, and it was not until I had to terminate my pregnancy at five months along that I questioned the relevance of my relationship with my faith. Reconciling that insurmountable suffering I had not been spared took me almost ten years, and I journeyed into the world of spiritual books, crystals, angel cards, chakra healing, yoga, astrology, color-therapy, numerology, psychosomatics, aromatherapy, and anything else I felt could help me. Again, while these were wonderful, it was not until I openly acknowledged and put extensive work into healing my childhood sexual traumas that I was able to make significant gains in solidifying my true spiritual self.

I also had to learn to re-parent and love the defiant seven-year-old girl that lives in my soul and to listen to her. She was first silenced by my grandfather's vile actions and secondly by the woman who had survived the abuse: me. I had once sworn the shame to secrecy, and in doing so had unknowingly made a deal with the devil. The serpent had whispered into my ear that I "would go to hell if I didn't obey" his wicked ways, and I had believed these lies because my survival depended on it. As a grown woman of wise mind, I have obviously rejected the notions of these venomous sermons he once preached and have finally managed to embrace the true goodness of grace, faith, and a loving God. I also honor the girl who endured the traumas and am entirely committed to loving her, and myself, unconditionally for the rest of my beautiful life because I deserve self-love.

Psychologically, I have been ensnared between life's dualities since the traumas happened…I wanted to be the "good girl" but have often felt the dark shadow taunting me to dance… maybe for the thrill? It was like I was in search of danger at all times, yet completely afraid of everything. I had once walked through what felt like the valley of the shadow of death, and still I feared the evil because my grandpa was a deviant predator who used any torture or lie necessary to achieve his goals, and yet I loved him.

The psychological term "splitting" relates to me, because in order to survive I could only focus on the "good grandpa" when I was growing up, and dissociatively forgave and forgot the rest. I had also adopted the "hunt or be hunted" attitude forever when it came to relationships, and it was only in remembering the abuse that I was able to identify where it came from. Grandpa and I had played the ultimate game of cat and mouse, and I really lost everything when he "won." It had been a silent world war of the wills, but the cards were obviously stacked in his favor as he was the predator, and I, as the defeated prey, blamed myself. I attribute a lot of my borderline traits, dissociative identity disorder, lichen sclerosus, depression, and complex stored trauma that have plagued me forever are related to and stem from his abuse. So, shame on him for causing these painful conditions.

Of course, there is no way to magically go back, but the experiences devastated my mind and body on so many different levels, for decades, that it changed me and rudely interrupted my natural journey into womanhood. The self-hatred the abuse caused was unbearable, and I had long projected that out into the world during stressful times throughout my life, and against myself.

Mentally, my brain has been on full speed, full time, trying to escape the memories of abuse and the hurt it caused me. I have suffered from not knowing what is real at times, because the girl in me protectively split from the trauma for over three decades in an attempt to deny and survive my life's ugliest truths. Ultimately, it took three breakdowns, and years of intensive psychotherapy, before I could safely face, let alone speak about, the memories that my seven-year-old self, had experienced at the hands of my delinquent grandfather, and before I could trust my memories to be valid.

The truth is, the abuse caused me to second guess everything in life, and I have struggled to find a healthy, solid ground in my own heart, head, and body ever since. My mental health has paid a dear price for the wrongful actions of my sinful grandfather, and my deepest depression and self-hatred were absolutely a direct result of the trauma he inflicted on my young self. My moods have been up and down my whole life because of the fear he instilled in me, and my emotional regulation has been weak when I am in crisis. Often my inner child acts out when I snap and "go to war" with others, which at times happens instantly, but I am always working on minimizing these feelings using logic.

Psychosomatically, I have been frozen in fear since the traumas happened and have spent a lot of time living in my head. As a child I experienced a lot of headaches, sometimes so bad I once saw auras and passed out at school. I had a weak immune system, allergies, asthma, and had even suffered the German measles shortly after the mononucleosis infection in Grade 2. My body often felt sluggish growing up, and my brain was sad, anxious, and obsessive. Once I got to high school, however, I was able to get a whole lot of what I wanted, and this seemed to excite me on some levels, but then I would go through a personal drama and would be back to wanting to be dead. As I went through my twenties and thirties, my body suffered with different kinds of painful ailments that ranged from severe sinus headaches to sore muscles and skin eruptions to a range of sexual and psychological issues.

During these years, I also felt allergic to my periods and pregnancies, likely for hormonal reasons or the lichen sclerosus. I experienced chronic fatigue, stiff muscles, struggled with TMJ, and was self-isolating by throwing myself into work, babies, and building our family life. However, it was not until after my last breakdown at the age of forty-two that I was finally able to recognize the trauma stored in my body, subconscious, or psychological makeup, and could begin to heal what my grandfather had obliterated so many years ago. Remedying these core wounds is a journey I expect to be on for the rest of my life, but one that I am willing to take armed with love, patience, mindfulness, kindness, sensitivity, and a soft yet powerful song. ❤

Eighteen

LET THERE BE LIGHT AND CHANGE

Going forward, what can communities do to help the countless survivors of incest and childhood sexual abuse? Perhaps, we should stop whispering or joking about abuses and start engaging in some meaningful conversations; consider putting an end to rape scenes in films; commit to reporting all sexual crimes against children; and softly encourage survivors to speak against the trauma they have experienced. These few things would all be some important actions that people everywhere would likely support.

In the future, I hope the world will learn to respectfully acknowledge, maybe even radically accept the fact incest abuse happens, and that children who are traumatized as a result are not freaks or disgusting. Incest is not a topic that should ever be joked about, especially in TV shows and movies, because it is simply rude. No survivors choose the abuse; and they were powerless over the experiences they were subjected to, so it is not fair to end every conversations about incest with, "That's disgusting" just because you think the topic is uncomfortable. The sad truth is, as survivors, all we silently hear is that we are disgusting, and this only perpetuates more shame within our secret. As culturally inappropriate as it is to joke about rape, the same thing needs to hold true for incest abuse, which often includes all forms of rape. This has too long been a closeted or taboo subject, and one that has led to a secret pandemic of hedonistic consequences, which affects the mental wellbeing of any children it infects, some who may never recover from the abuse.

I have read old statistics that as many as 1 out of 20 dads may be incestuously harming their own children, and the number increases to 1 out of 7 when stepfathers are involved. (1) Even if these are inaccurate, replace the word dad with; grandpa, cousin, babysitter, sibling, coach, or religious leader and the numbers add up quickly. The truth is anyone can be a serial predator, so be cautious at all times. Caregivers, also be extra mindful when playing the "he would never" game! It is dangerous, and one in which your child has everything to lose. In fact, large numbers of people, including celebrities who are diagnosed with BPD, CPTSD, dissociative identity disorder, addictions, eating disorders, and those who self-harm or die by suicide, often have histories of being sexually abused, harmed, or traumatized as children.

As a society we must learn to be less judgmental about mental-health issues and start asking what is the root cause of our own or others' inner battles? How can we heal? How can we help those we love? Also, consider if your perfect child just "changes" one day, out of the blue: open your eyes to any abuse they may have experienced because there is no "take back" on virginity or abuse. The child will need psychiatric care, maybe a medical evaluation, or to work with a school counselor at the very least if they have been harmed, because just pretending abuse does not happen hurts us all. So, keep the blinders of denials off and remain absolutely sensitive to your child's need for personal and sexual safety.

Something Hollywood could do to help end toxic rape culture is to stop subjecting viewers to any more rape scenes in films or shows. Think about this. Most consumers watching the program can already imagine how bad a rape would feel, but for those of us who repeatedly lost the battle to our attacker, we know exactly how bad the violence and rape feels. So whatever sadistic, rape, fetish, or Freudian fantasies the producers are trying to sell, they simply are not sexy. I likely speak for most people and all survivors when I say please STOP. Nobody enjoys being subjected to these images of sexually brutalizing women on the big screen. As a consumer, I no longer even buy tickets to shows I know contain rape scenes because of the element of feeling traumatized after the movie.

The men who protect and empower their partners or families also have a huge role to play in the future safety of our children. Bless the good ones who stand by us no matter what and who crawl around in the trenches to help us lovingly raise our children and keep us grounded. Men are not the problem in society, only predators are, because "real" men do not sexually harm children, and they need to be valued for the powerful love that they can bring to a healthy family unit. The good-hearted men encourage us to seek justice for sexual crimes or to heal the damage caused by it, and they are true heroes. Husbands, sons, brothers, help us speak against the plague of toxic masculinity that has prevailed for far too long, and cheerlead the change you wish to see for your children, mothers, sisters, daughters, or anyone else you love. Most importantly, if you witness predatory actions perpetrated by others, call it out or report it. If you see something abusive or perverse happening to a person you love, speak up. Right away, because it is always the right thing to do if you want to serve your beloved community of women and children well. Additionally, if you as a male have been preyed upon, it is also your right to speak against your attacker without shame, and families should fiercely support this.

Friends and family can help by gently encouraging anyone who has been sexually harmed to find therapeutic support for mental health issues, especially a child who has been through any level of sexual abuse. I promise you; they have been affected and may need prescription medication, trauma counseling, and possibly medical care. If you are the parent or confidant of a survivor and they disclose abuse, the first thing to do is remain calm. While the shocking news may be heartbreaking and leave you wanting to lash out at the perpetrator, the survivor's best shot at recovery will be how well you manage the disclosure, so keep your emotions in check.

Secondly, put on your best, non-judgmental listening ears, hear the full story, and then tell your loved one you are terribly sorry that happened to them. Tell them you believe them. Offer them comfort, and then get straight to work finding ways to heal the trauma caused by the predator.

Pretending childhood sexual abuse, rape, or incest does not happen impacts the world as a whole and it can only breed more shame, secrecy, and criminality by staying silent. Please, call out the predators, prosecute them, and do not be afraid to ruin their fake "good" reputation. One important thing I have come to terms with is that the second the abuse started, the stories became mine to tell, and if my grandfather did not want the "bad press," he should have kept his filthy hands, mouth, and body away from me, period. Anyone who knew my grandfather might proclaim he had lovable qualities, and I believe he did too, but I can't ignore the abuse out of toxic loyalty.

I admit he was financially generous with everyone, passionate, musical, playful, funny, superficially charming, and a self-proclaimed, "Man of God," but it wasn't until I revisited blocked childhood memories that I was able to clearly see the monster behind his madness. So, ruin his life? I wonder if he ever considered how the abuse might weaponize life's most intimate acts for me and destroy my ability to ever feel safe. The truth is, he had zero empathy, or his insatiable ego would not have feasted on my innocence with such a deranged entitlement. Now he is dead, and he never faced allegations or prosecution for his violent sexual crimes, so I feel he got away easy. As a grandpa, he had one job to do, which was to protect me from harm, and I fully expected him to do exactly that. Instead, his abuse negatively impacted my sanity for almost thirty-five years, plus an additional four years in therapy healing from the fear he instilled in me and trying to regain the personal safety he robbed me of decades ago.

I suspect some of my family may stand delusional, "innocent," or loyal with Grandpa's code of silence and "deny, deny, deny," or maybe they do not remember any abuse. I will love them anyway, but it is also my right to bravely stand up and acknowledge his perverse betrayals to the love we gave him and the grace I gave him. Either way, I have stood alone with this secret since I was seven and will continue to do so with or without the validation of anyone. (However, if any friends or family may have also experienced child sexual abuse by my grandfather, I am deeply sorry for the pain he caused, and sorry that I could not process or articulate the abuse sooner. If he harmed you, I encourage you to give voice to the abuses and seek psychiatric help, because he was a particularly dangerous and deeply disturbed predator from my recollection of personal experiences.)

For the countless warriors who have survived sexual abuse, rapes, incest, or any other intrusions, trust me when I say I understand the vacancy of love in your heart and the rage that lives in your soul. I can relate to your pain and your traumas because I lived through sexual abuse, and I know how destructive it can be on our core self. Hear me when I say you are not alone and that I am deeply sorry for the trauma you once experienced. I am sorry if nobody noticed your pain, you were not believed when you told somebody, you did not have the language necessary to tell the story, or you were just too terrified to speak against your abuser at such a tender young age, as I once was. I ask you to forgive yourself now, pledge to ending your self-harm or self-criticism, and I warmly encourage you to take a journey towards healing your own psychological wounds, because we are all worthy of healthy self-love. Please reach out for help with mental health issues if you haven't already, eat well, play well, do work you enjoy, write, read, spend time in nature, lead with love in your relationships, and take charge of the beautiful life you were given, because you get to script the rest of your story! ❤

Hopefully my intimate recount of life events has helped you gain some insights about how cunningly incest abuses happen, why children often fail to speak up, how the abuse affects a child's mental health, development and personality, and maybe even why bringing awareness to this often-dismissed subject matter is so very important. Maybe your life depends on it, or maybe your child's or a child you love, or a grandchild's. Either way, we cannot afford any more secret abuses, so keep the lines of communication open with young people about their sexual safety and teach them to voice any harms they may experience because speaking up is always the right thing to do.

Survivors stories matter, and it is up to us to get a simple message out there: no more secrecy. If you are reading this book and being sexually abused, or a loved one is being harmed, report the crimes as quickly as it is safe to do so. Society has protected the perpetrators of these wrongdoings for centuries by staying silent, and we need to all rebel against the secrecy if we are to ever break the cycle of sexual violence that is happening within our own families and to our innocent children. They are our bright future, and they deserve one free from the extensive predatory harms caused by shameful childhood sexual abuse, especially by a family member.

My closing wishes for the many readers who have experienced sexual traumas, are that you learn to sing your unique song, begin to mend the core wounds abuse creates, find a way to turn your silenced pain into a powerful passion, and eventually, design a purposeful life that is yours to live as loudly as you please! Proudly, and free from all shame. Healing is the long, brave journey we take, making recovery the holy grail. ❤

#songoversilence

GRATITUDES...

First, and foremost, thank you to my twenty-four-year ride or die partner and better half, Dusten. Your friendship, stability, focus, light sense of humor, protective nature, commitment, and love have all been driving forces in my life. Thank you for your patience, for raising Owen plus our own sweet, hypersensitive children with me with an open heart, and for refusing to ever give up on our family.

My wonderful children, thank you for bringing light into my life, and for loving me through the process of trying to learn how to love myself. You three have brought me great joy, softened my heart, and made me a better woman, and I am forever indebted to you for the compassion you have granted me as a mother. You have been my reasons to fight to survive in a complex world that was interrupted by trauma and to finally speak out against childhood sexual abuse so that our family may lead with a legacy of light instead of darkness.

Extra special thanks to my mom for loving me through the storms I have called life. I love her for being a strong female role model to our family, for her grounded nature, her humor, her thoughtfulness, her decades of care, her wisdom, her passion for reading, and for creating four powerful daughters. Beneath all that strength lies a softhearted woman who always wants the best for the ones she calls family, and we adore her for being such a wonderful grandma!

Thank you to my dad for teaching me how to be a "man," how to push back against bullies, how to work hard, how to chase big dreams, to be independent, to believe in myself, to make money, and most importantly how to survive in a "man's" world. These gifts allowed me success in a male-dominated sector of agriculture, and I love him forever for the privilege of being his "daughter number one." He was my best friend, business partner, mentor, and a man who loved his family more than anything. I am thankful to have known and loved him and to have called him my dad.

My dear sisters, thank you for putting up with all my wildness over the decades and for growing into a tribe of such incredible women. I love you three more than I could ever show you and am proud of the work you do—most importantly, how you are raising your children. Empathy, compassion, strength, patience, unconditional love, and giving them a voice are some of the greatest lessons you will ever teach. I adore you, girls, and I bless your journeys of motherhood.

Paula, Susan, and my dear mother-in-law, Deborah, you have been the best friends a girl could ever ask for. You have loved me unconditionally, listened to my chatter, held empathetic space for me, validated my stories, checked on me when I needed it, and encouraged me to write this book. Thank you for sharing your stories with me and for letting me know that I am not a lone survivor. Also, Connie, Penni, and Anne for decades of timeless friendships. Angie, thank you for the beautiful hair styling and friendship all these years.

Thank you to my local mental health professionals for providing all my psychiatric services and therapy for over four years. This healing process has been an incredible journey into reconciling my womanhood and one I could not have done without the resources they offered.

FriesenPress Inc., thank you for all the publishing services you have provided and your valued support!

(A fangirl thank you to Dr. Brené Brown for her book, *Rising Strong*. I read it when I was "face down in the arena," and it inspired a manuscript idea titled "owning my story." Your BRAVING strategy, plus books and clarity about the importance of facing shame, changed my life.

Also, a musical shout out to Kesha for her song "Praying" because it was my theme song while writing this book, and it gave me strength and power during my darkest days of recovery. Thank you for your courage to speak truth to power, and for your beats.

Lastly, Gretchen Carlson and Megyn Kelly for their bravery in being women who lead. You ladies are the bombs! #bombshellmovie)

REFERENCES AND RESOURCES

Adams, Douglas Carlton, the Dali Lama, and the Archbishop Desmond Tutu. *The Book of Joy*. New York: Viking Press, 2016.

Allendar, Dan B. *Healing the Wounded Heart*: *The Heartache of Sexual Abuse and the Hope for Transformation.* Michigan: Baker Publishing Group, 2016.

Angelou, Maya. *I Know Why the Caged Bird Sings*. New York City: Random House, 1969.

Baron-Cohen, Simon. *The Science of Evil: On Empathy and the Origins of Cruelty*. New York: Basic Books, 2014.

Brizendine, Louann. *The Female Brain*. New York: Harmony, 2007.

Brown, Brené. *Daring Greatly*: *How the Courage to be Vulnerable Transforms the Way We Live, Love, Parent, and Lead*. New York: Avery, 2012.

Brown, Brené. *Rising Strong: How the Ability to Reset Transforms the Way We Live, Love, Parent and Lead*. New York: Spiegel & Grau, 2015.

Chemaly, Soraya. *Rage Becomes Her: The Power of Women's Anger*. New York: Atria Books, 2018.

DSM-5. The American Psychiatric Association. New York: 2013.

Hanh, Thich Nhat. *The Art of Living: Peace and Freedom in Here and Now*. New York: Harper Collin, 2017.

Hemingway, Mariel. *Out Came the Sun: Overcoming the Legacy of Mental Illness, Addiction, and Suicide in my Family*. New York: Regan Arts, 2015.

James, Laura. *Odd Girl Out: My Extraordinary Autistic Life*. New York: Seal Press, 2018.

Kreisman, Gerald J, and Straus, Hal. *I Hate You- Don't Leave Me*. New York: TarcherPerigee, 2012.

Shapiro, Francine. *Getting Past Your Past: Take Control of Your Life with Self-Help Techniques from EMDR Therapy*. Pennsylvania: Rodale Books, 2012.

Smith, Anne W. *Overcoming Perfectionism: Finding the Key to Balance and Self-Acceptance*. Deerfield Beach: Health Communications Inc, 2013.

Stevens, Michelle. *Scared Selfless: My Journey from Abuse and Madness to Surviving and Thriving.* New York: G.P. Putnam's Sons, 2017.

Strauss, Neil. *The Truth: An Uncomfortable Book About Relationships.* New York: Dey Street Books, 2015.

Van der Kolk, Bessel. *The Body Keeps the Score: Brain, Mind, and Body in the Healing of Trauma.* New York: Viking, 2014.

Walker, Pete. *Complex PTSD: From Surviving to Thriving.* South Valley: Create Space, 2016.

Wiley. E Sue Blume. *Secret Survivors: Uncovering Incest and Its Aftereffects in Women.* New York: Ballantine Books, 1990

(1) Kluft, Richard, P. Ramifications of Incest article January 11, 2011. Volume 27 Issue 12, https://psych iatrictimes.com/view/ramifications-incest

Film Credentials

Bryant, Lisa, dir. *Filthy Rich: A Powerful Billionaire, the Sex Scandal that Undid Him, and all the Justice Money Can Buy: The Shocking True Story of Jeffrey Epstein.* (4 Part Series) Radical Media. Aired May 10, 2020 on Netflix 55-57 min. https://www.netflix.com

Cohen, Bonnie and Shenk, Jon, dir. *Athlete A.* Actual films. Aired June 24, 2020 on Netflix, 104 min. https://www.athleteafilm.com

Fox, Jennifer, dir. *The Tale*, Gamechanger Films, Home Box Office (HBO) Aired May 26, 2018 on HBO, 114 min. https://www.thetalemovie.com

Oprah Winfrey Presents, "Leaving Neverland," Oprah Winfrey Network, Season 1, Episode 101. Home Box Office (HBO) Aired on March 04, 2019, on HBO, 58 min. https://www.oprah.com

Reed, Dan, dir. *Leaving Neverland.* Amos Pictures, Channel 4, Home Box Office (HBO). Aired March 3-4, 2019, on HBO, 240 min. https://www.hbo.com/documentaries/leaving-neverland

Rape, Abuse, and Incest National Network website, better known as RAINN https://rainn.org

Children's Help Phone 1-800-668-6868

Apple News, and Google for articles, YouTube for videos

songoversilence.com

@songoversilence on Instagram for Author photos, videos and TextArt

*Disclaimer: My memories are imperfect. However, I am sharing them to the best of knowledge, and I have changed any identifiers of all characters to protect people's privacy. (I am not a therapist, nor a lawyer)

The real-life members of my family portrayed in this story have always been loving and supportive of me throughout the years, and I adore them all. I recognize that their memories of the events described in this book are different than my own and wholeheartedly respect that. They are each bright, hard-working people and I want them to know that I loved growing up around such an amazing family. As such, this book is not intended to hurt anyone, but rather to shed light on a dark secret past based on my personal experiences alone. ❤

CPSIA information can be obtained
at www.ICGtesting.com
Printed in the USA
BVHW030624160521
607404BV00001B/17

9 781525 570421